A simple review on amazon really helps us out. So if you Could take one minut of yout time to leave one ,we would really appreciate that.
And thank you so much for your purchase .

COPYRIGHT © 2020 BY RED CRAFT

All rights reserved. No part of this publication may be reproduced, distributed, or transmitted in any form or by any means, including photocopying, recording, or other electronic or mechanical methods, without the prior written permission of the publisher, except in the case of brief quotations embodied in critical reviews and certain other noncommercial uses permitted by copyright law.

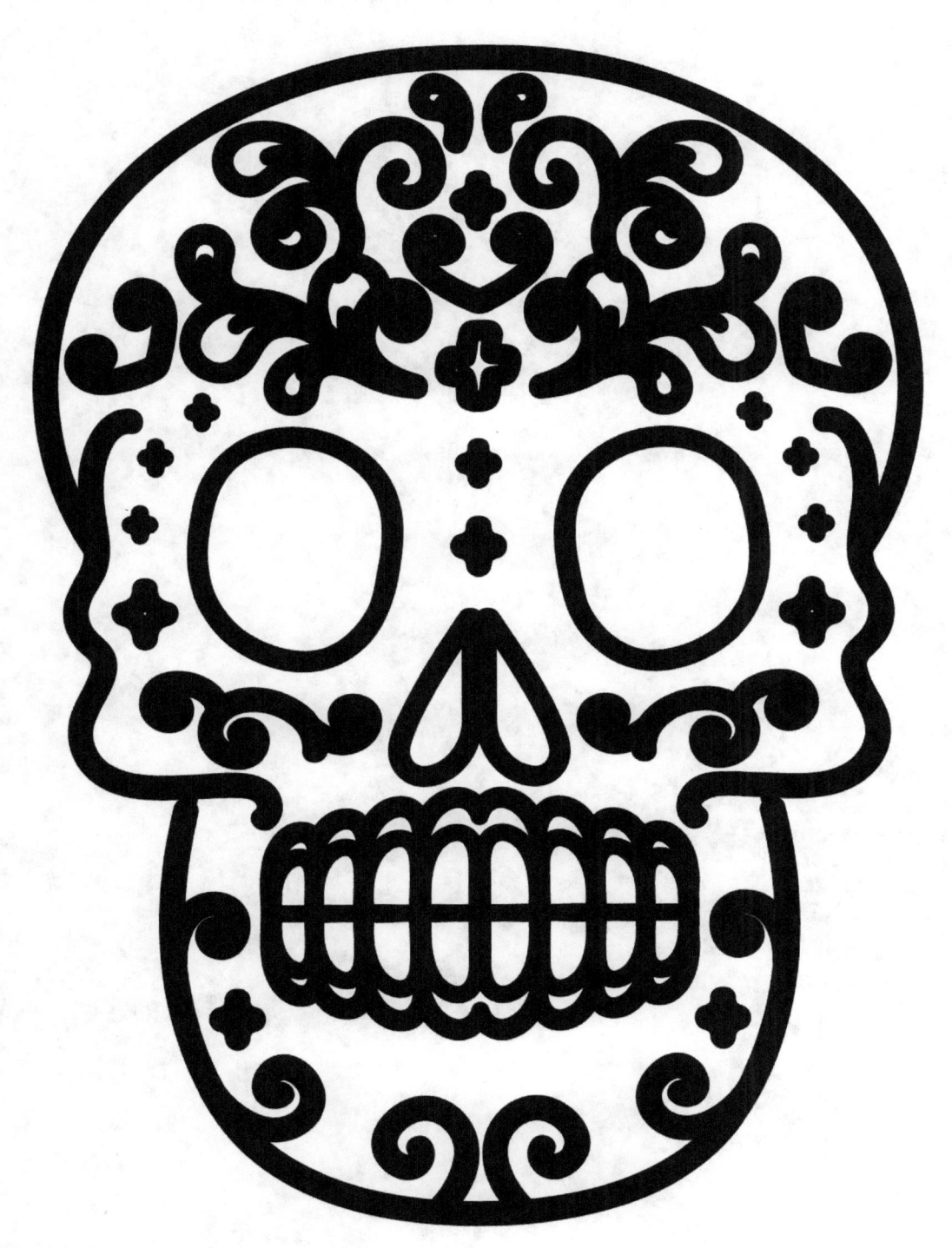

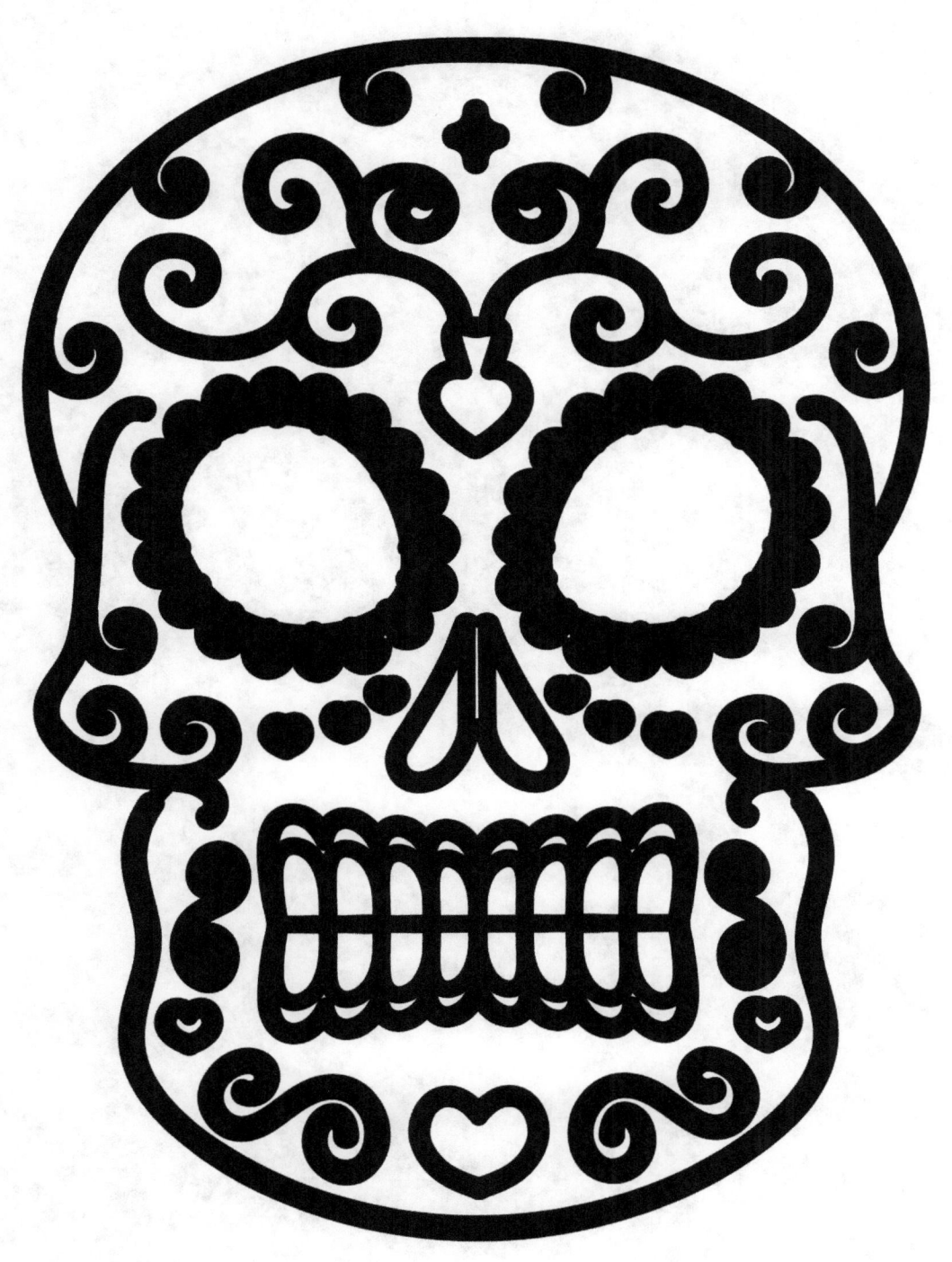

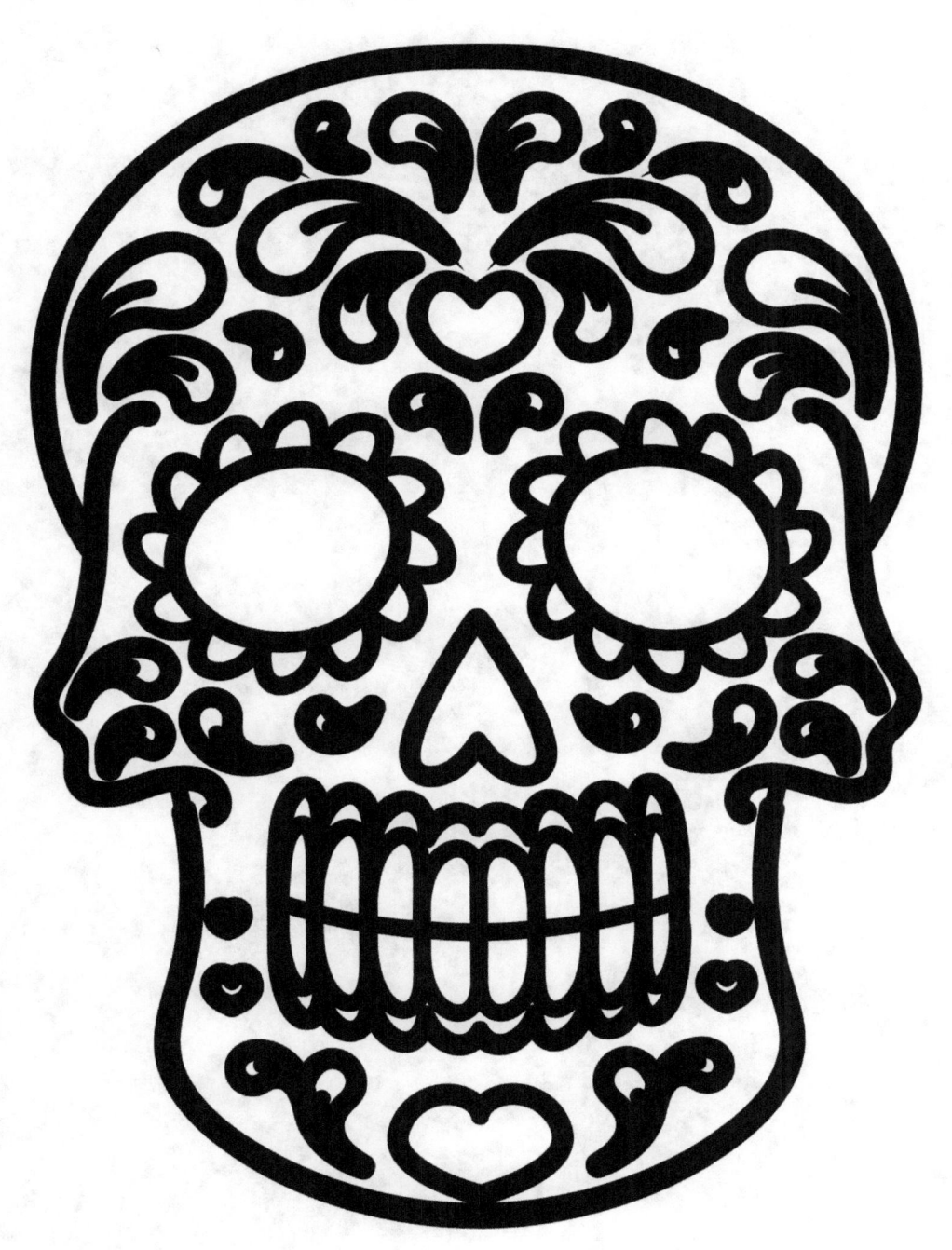

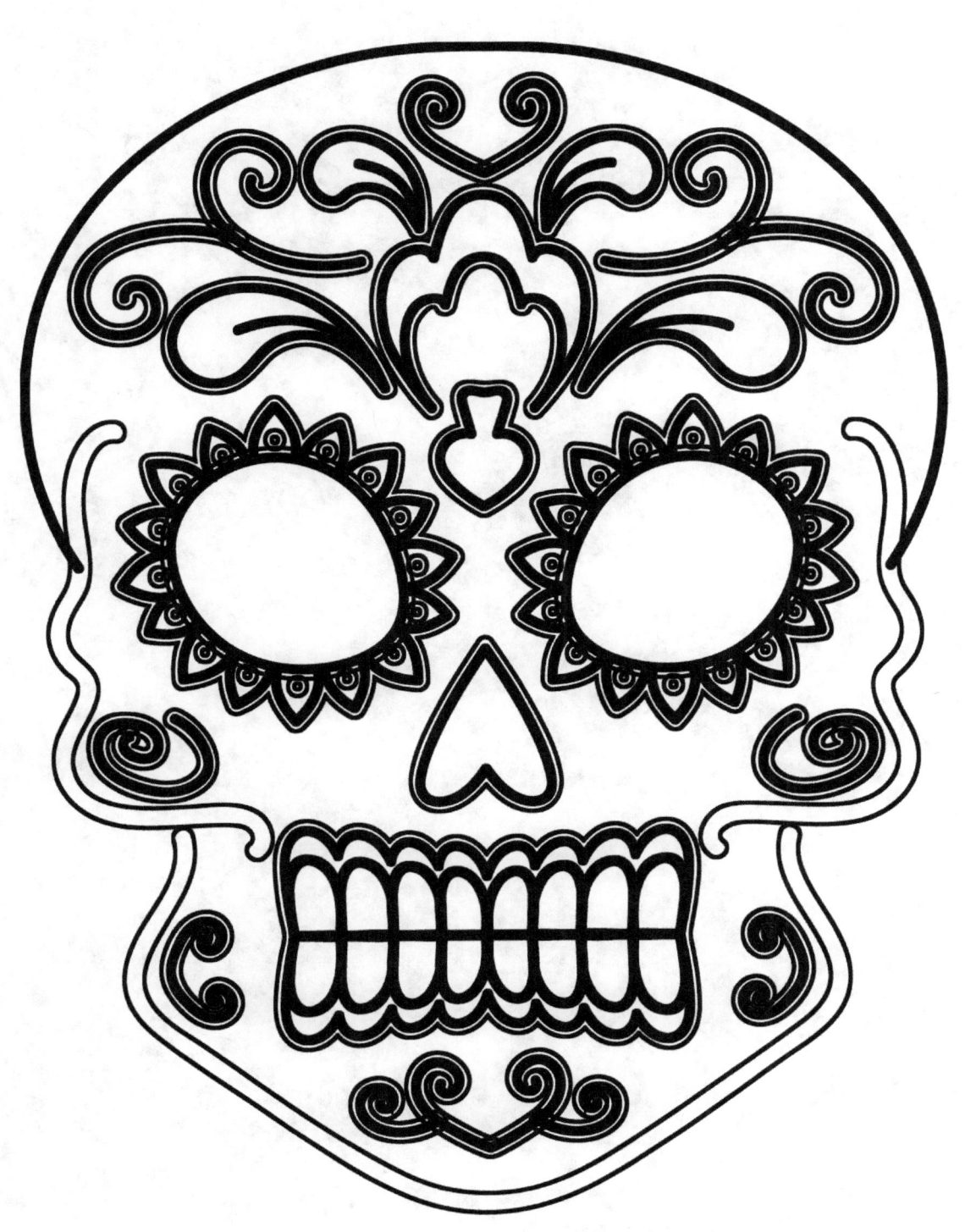

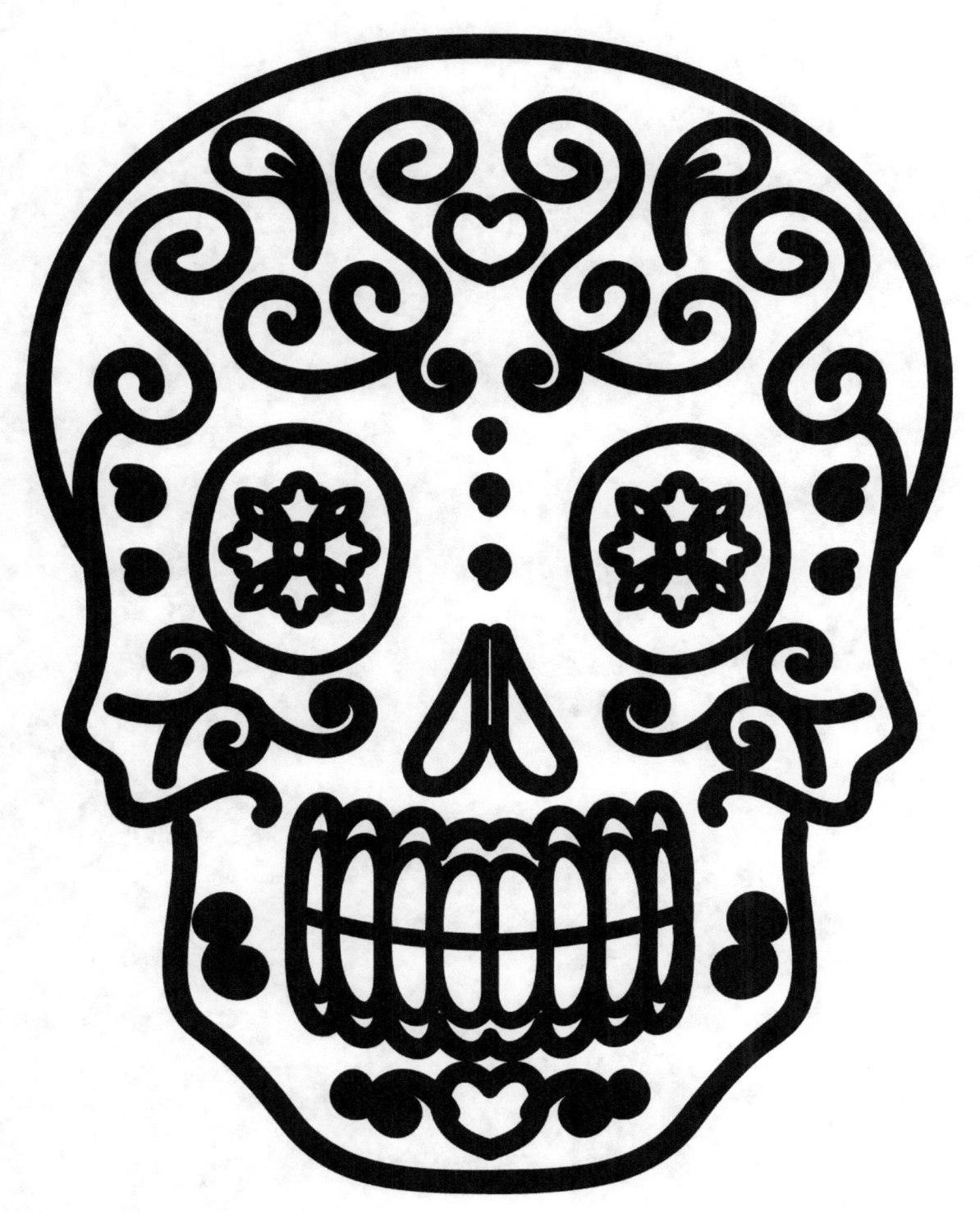

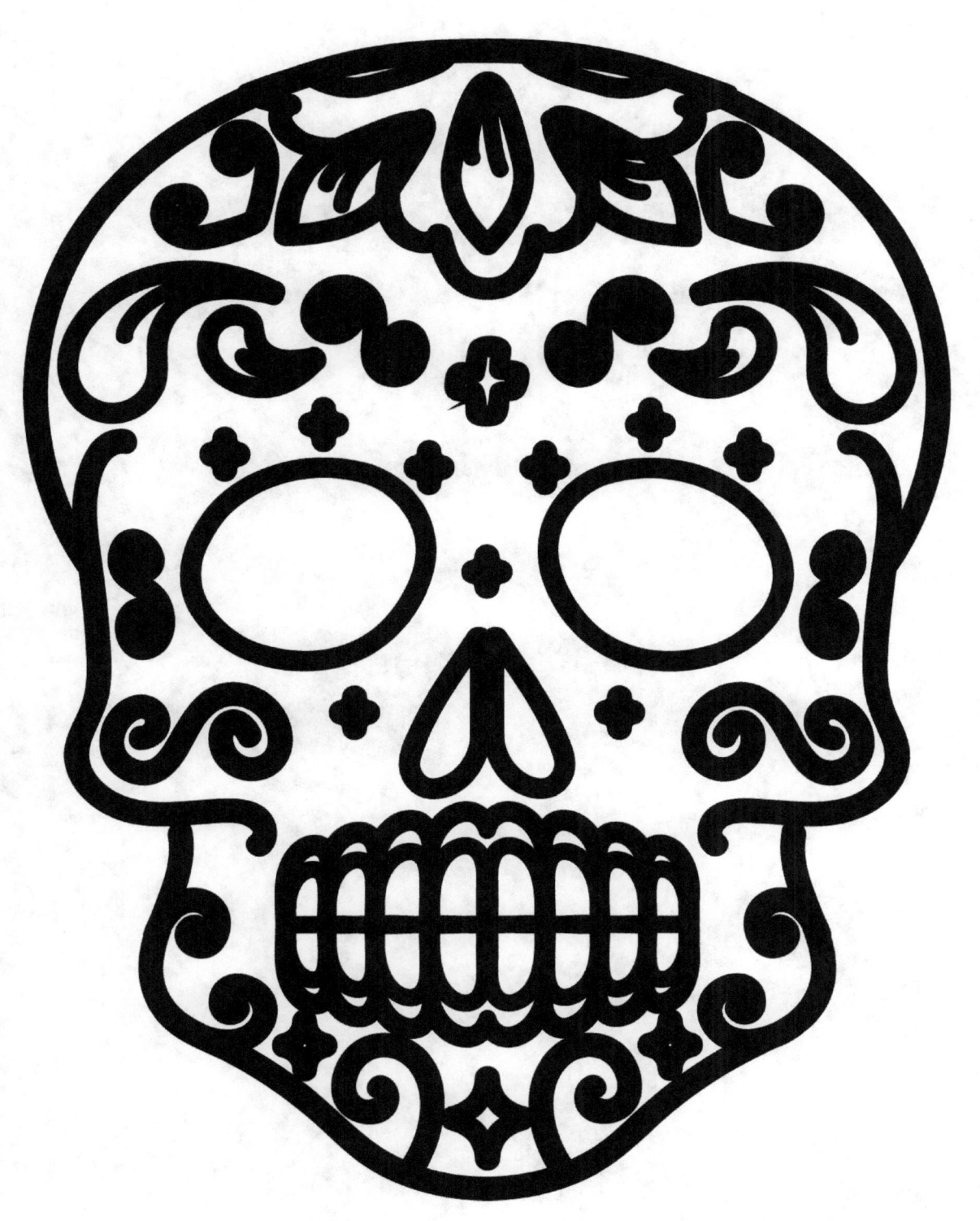

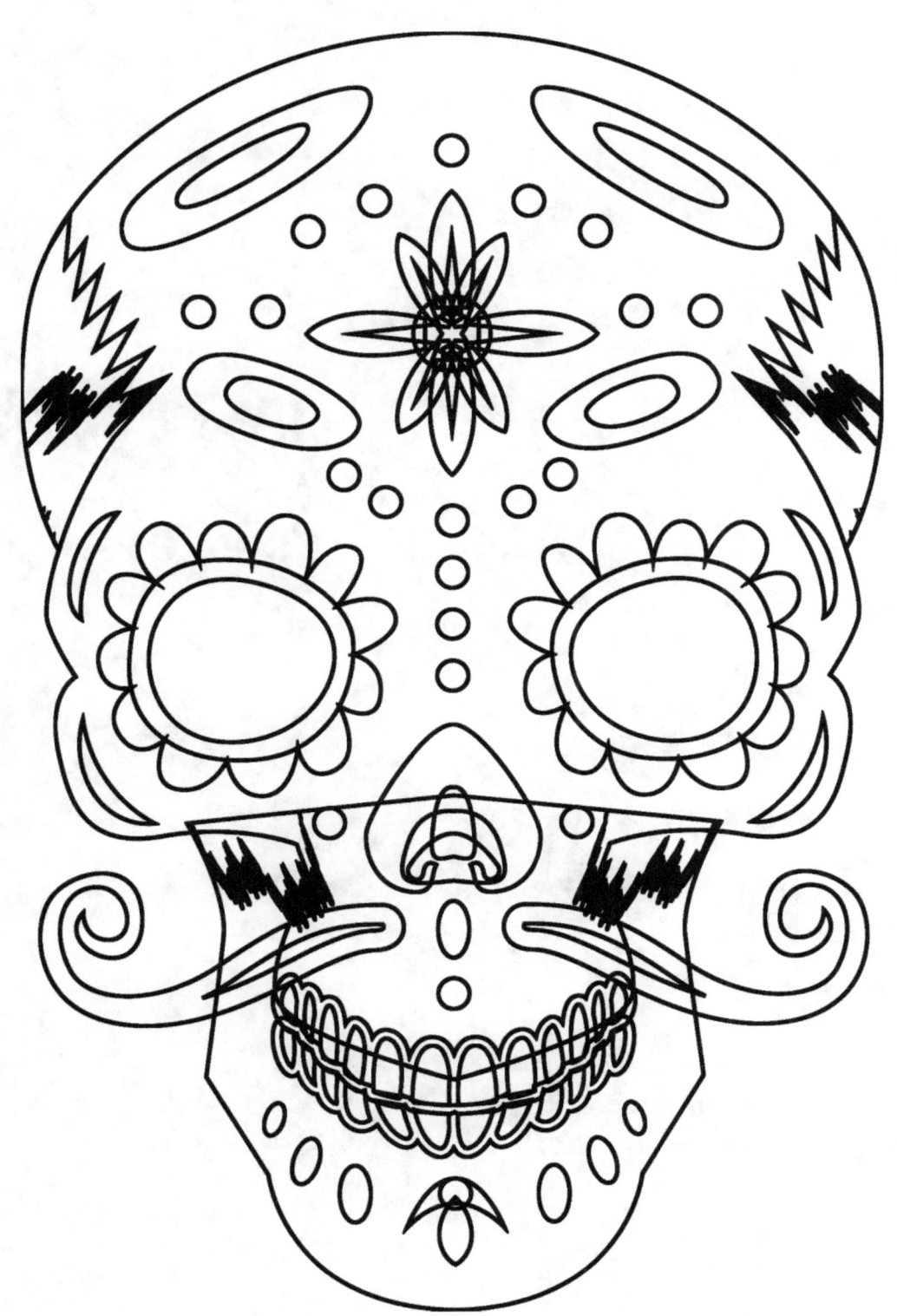

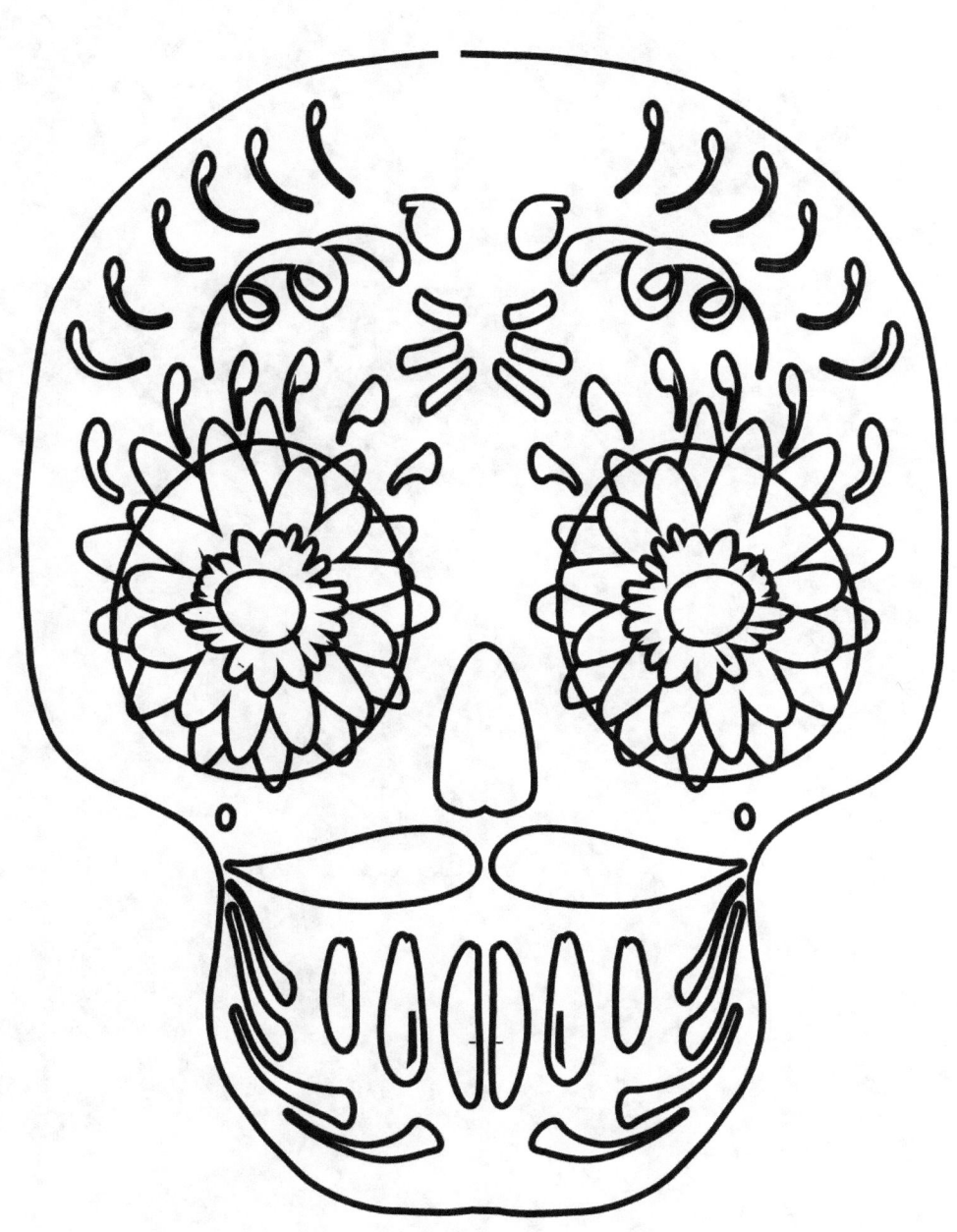

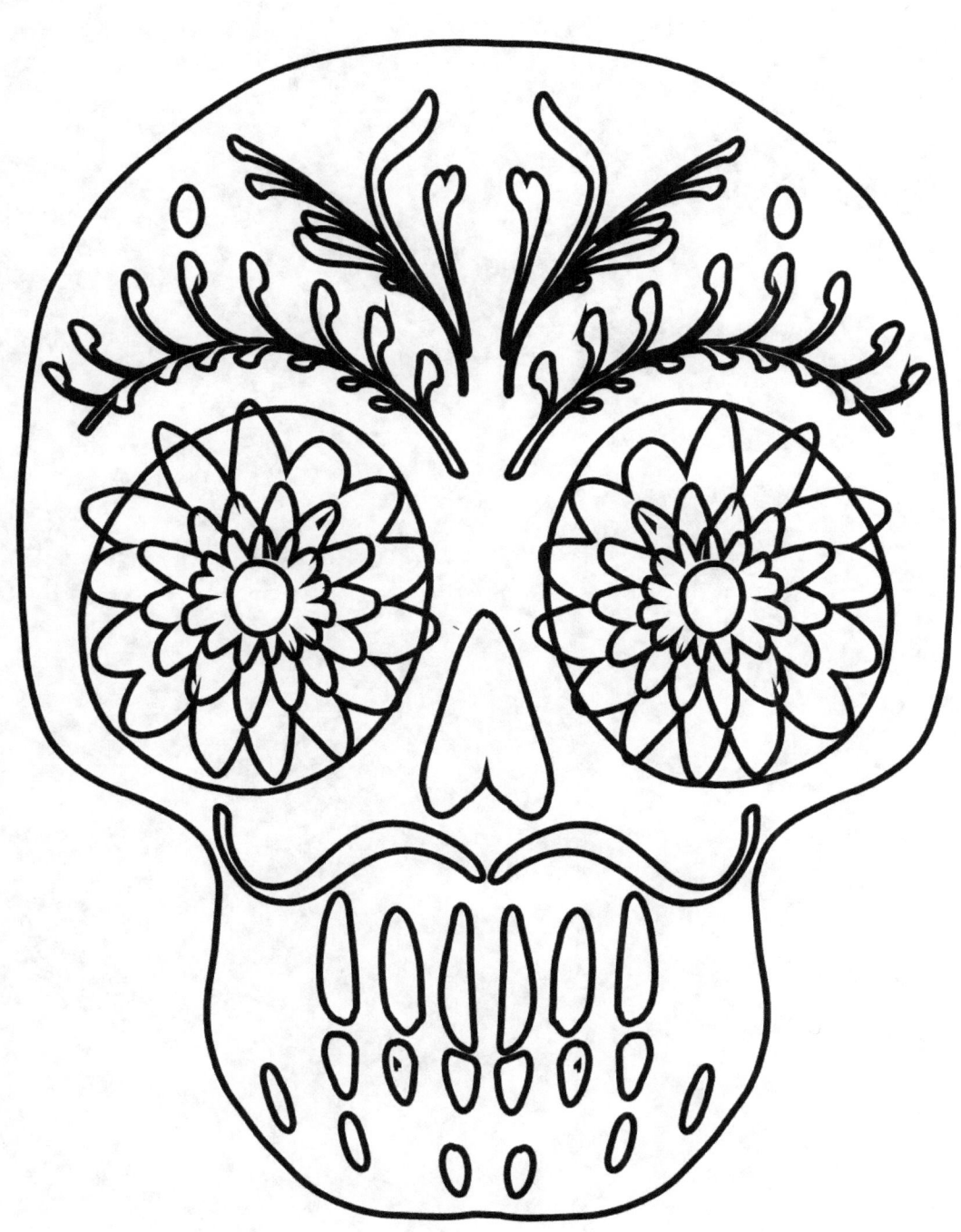

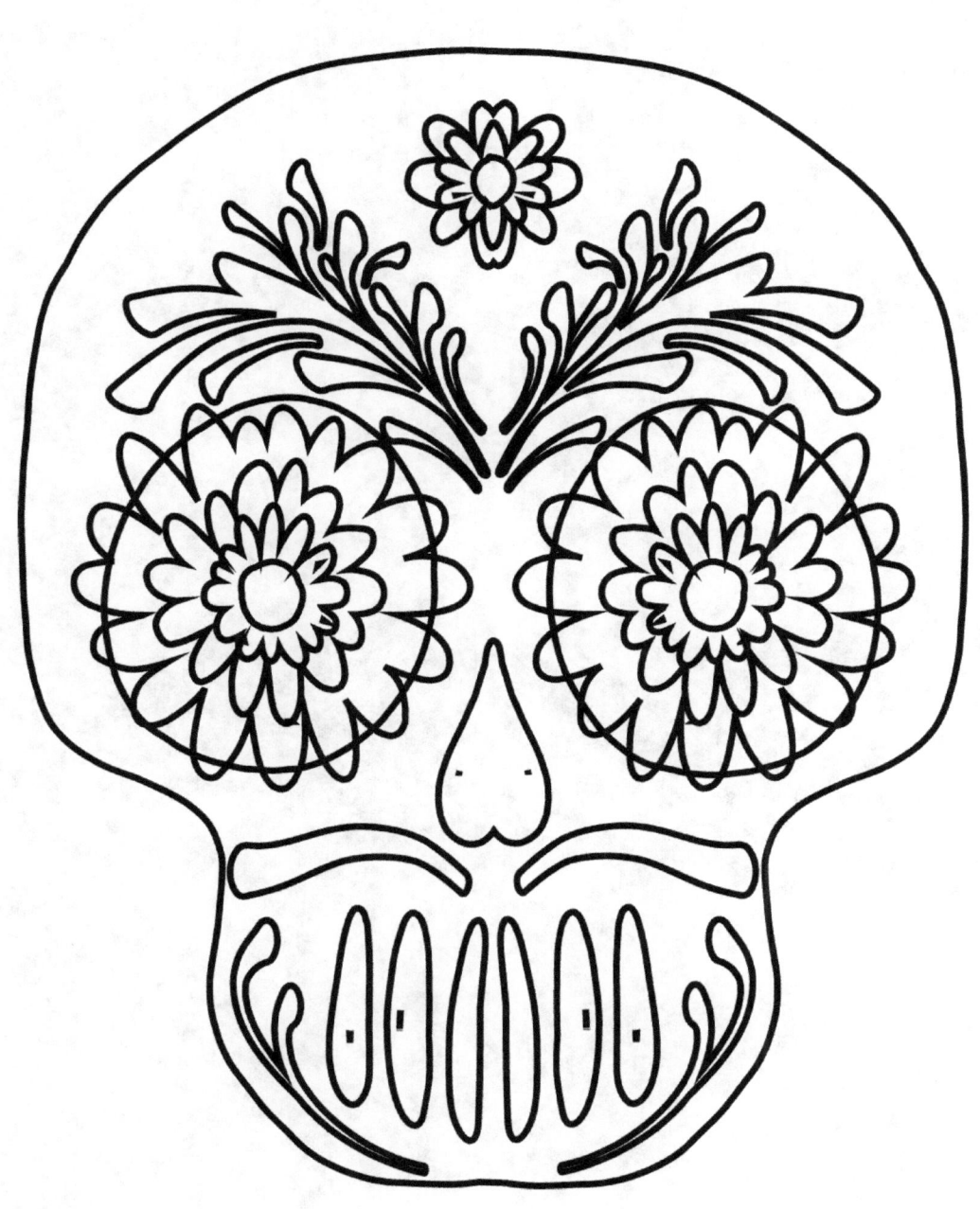

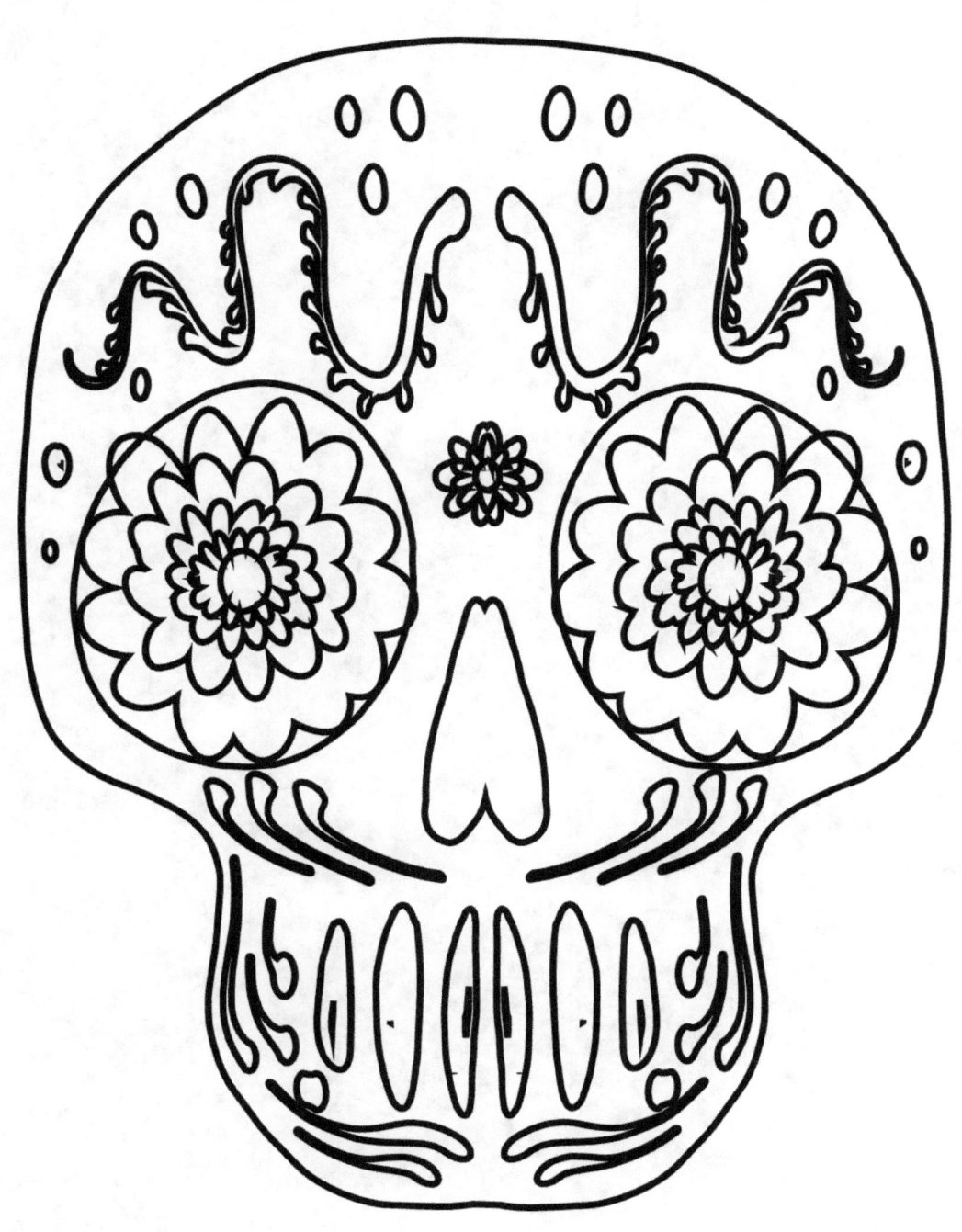

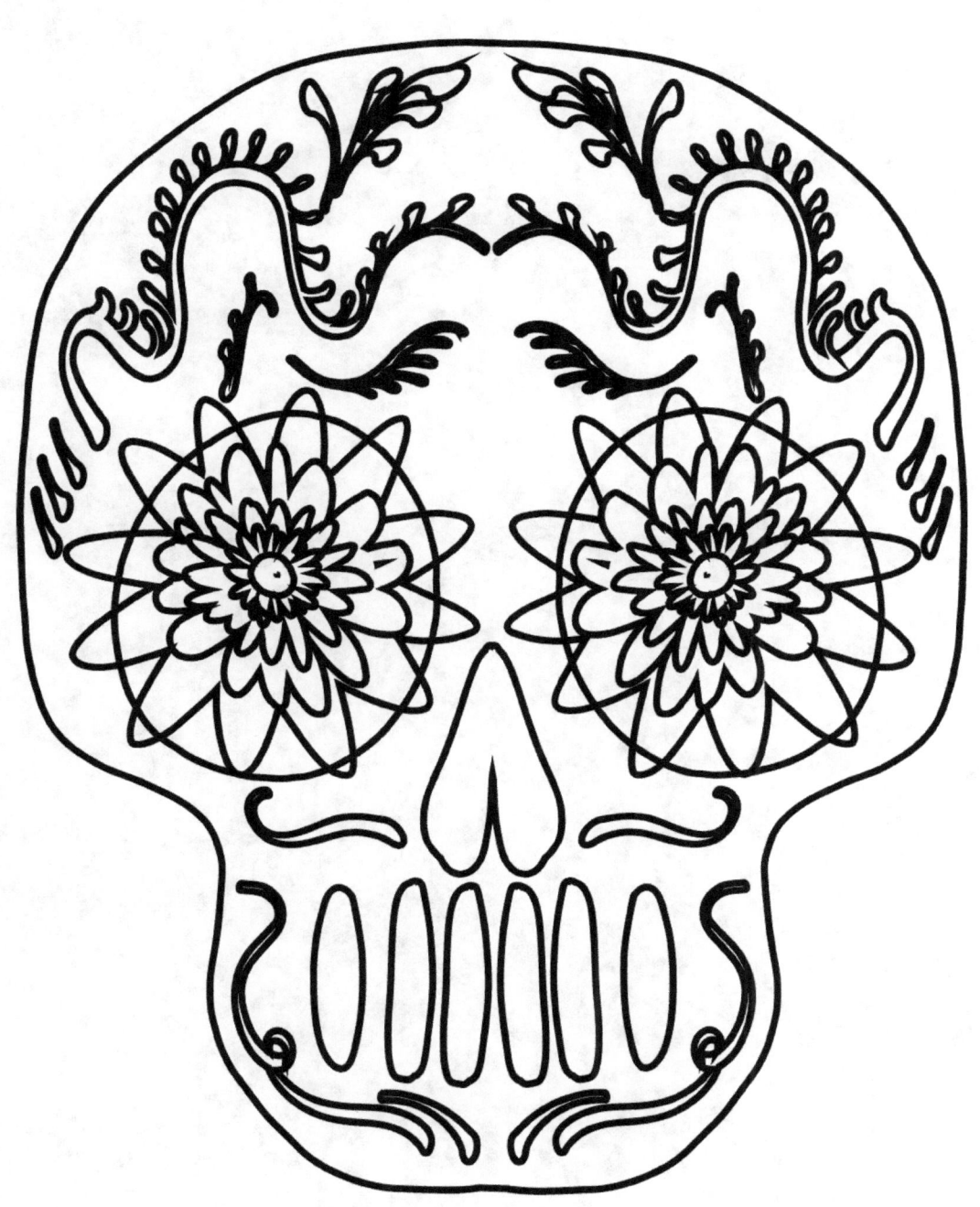

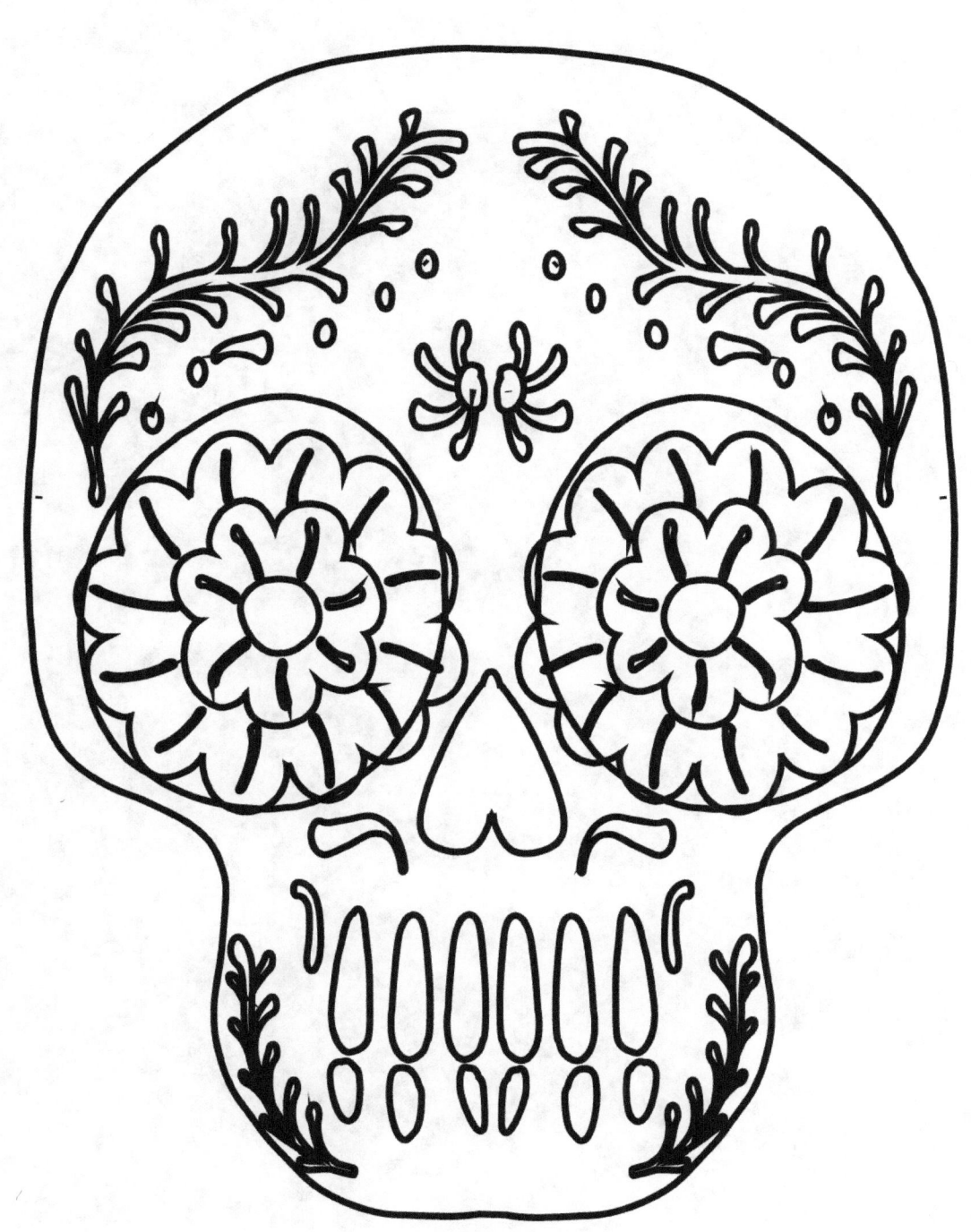

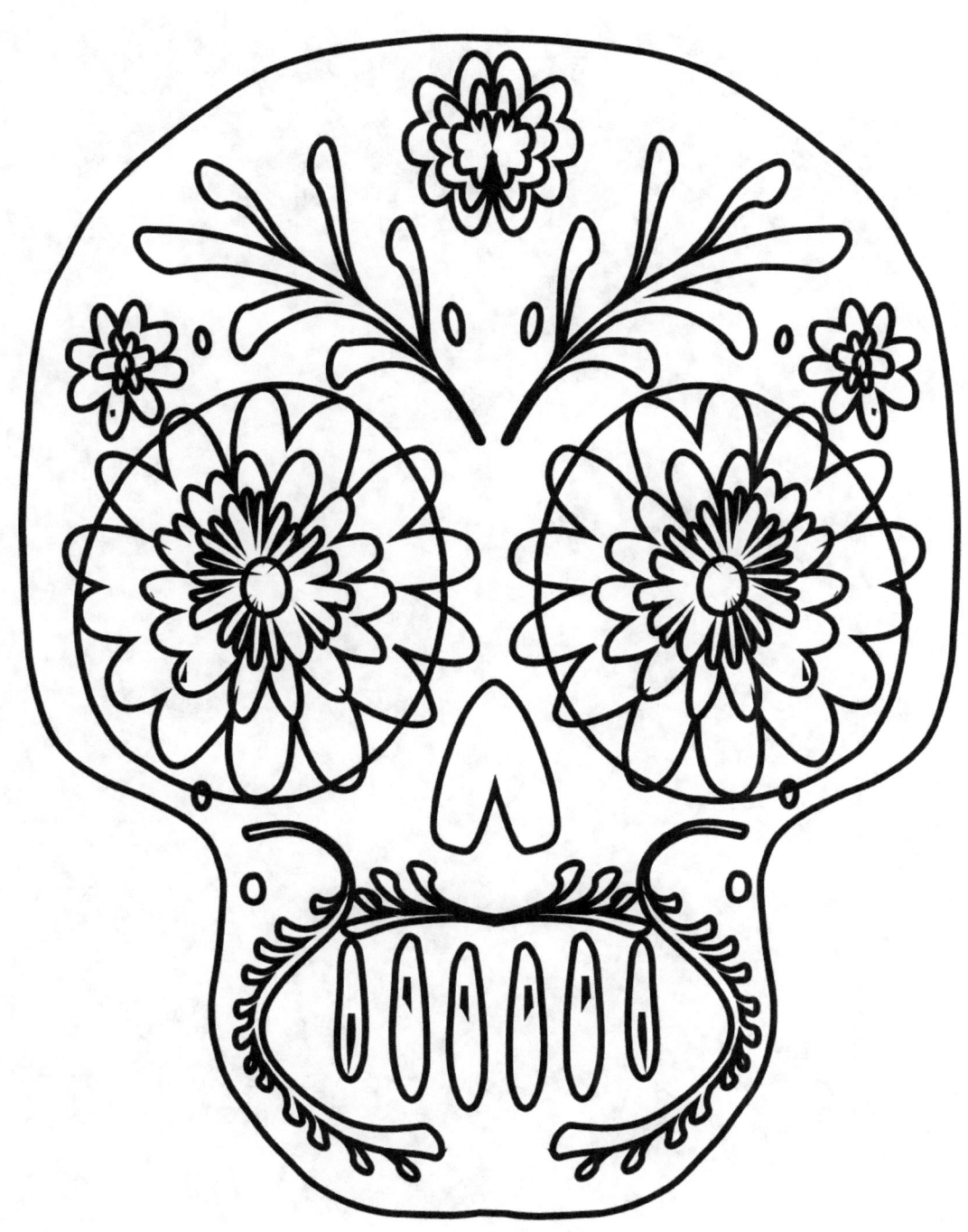

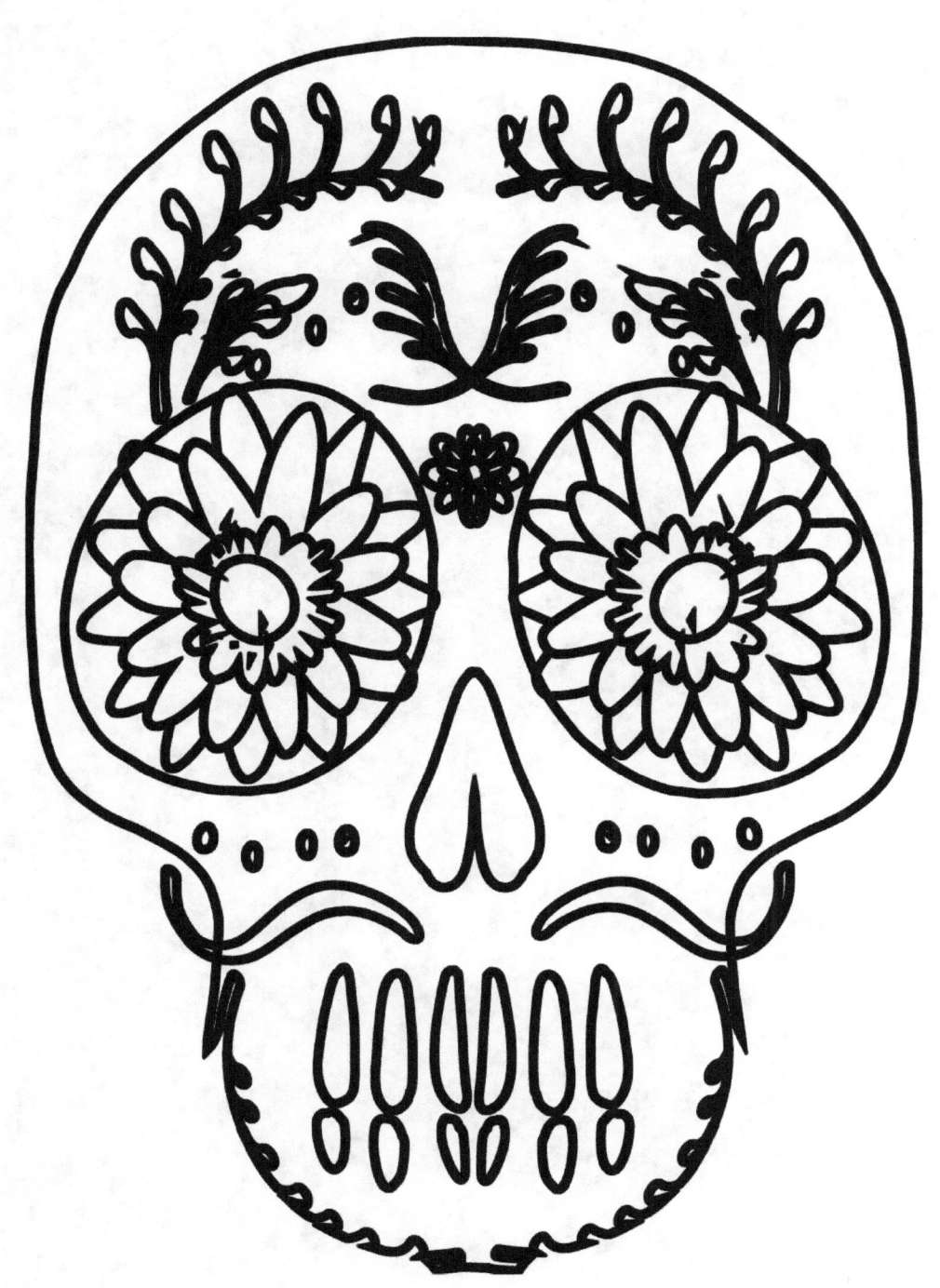

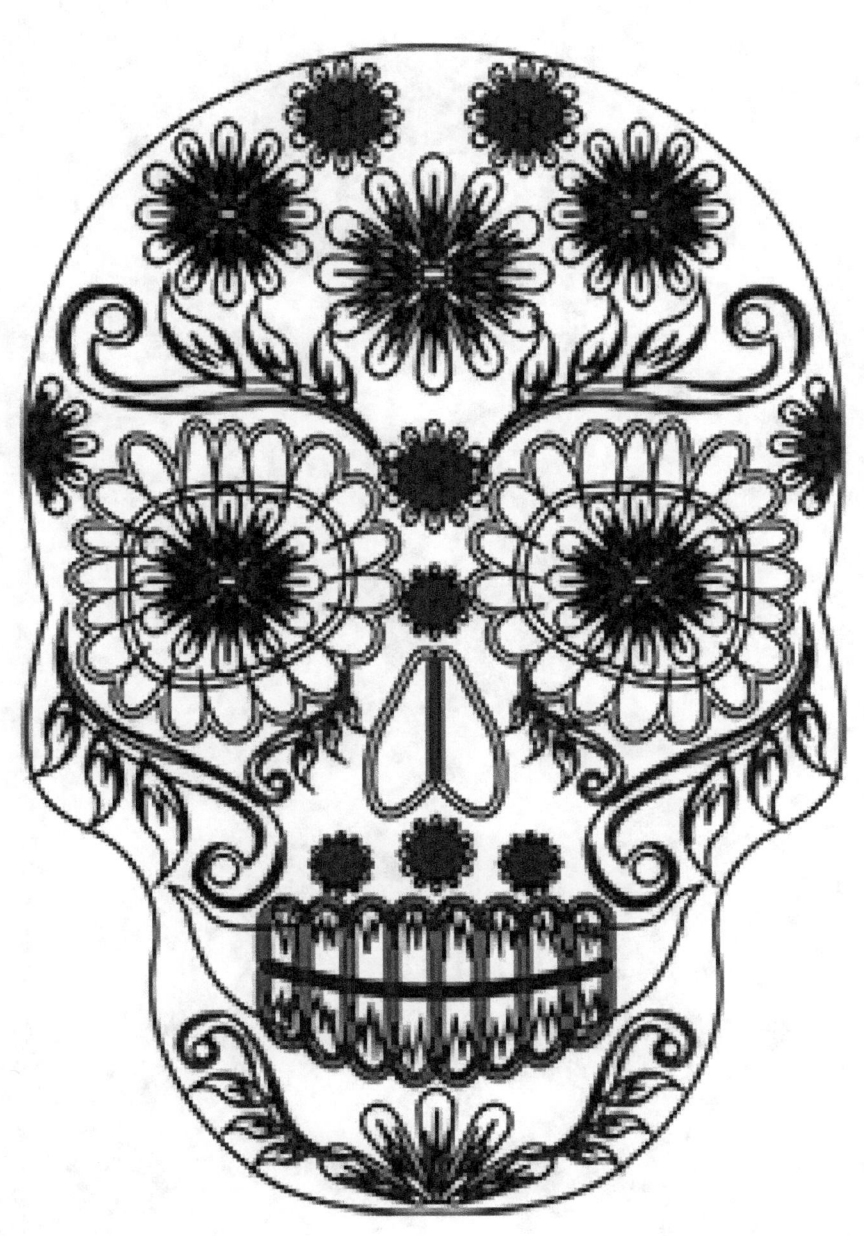

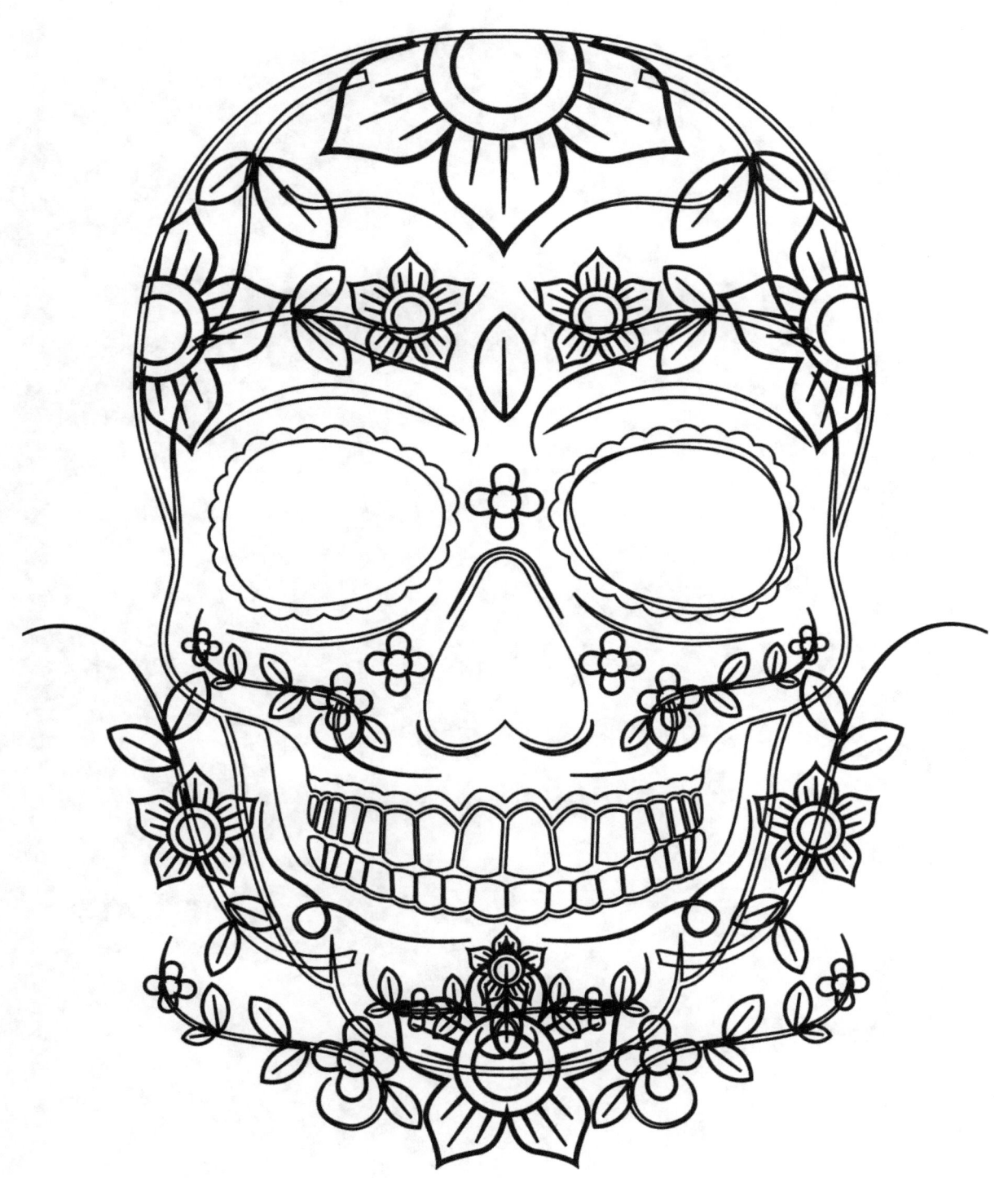

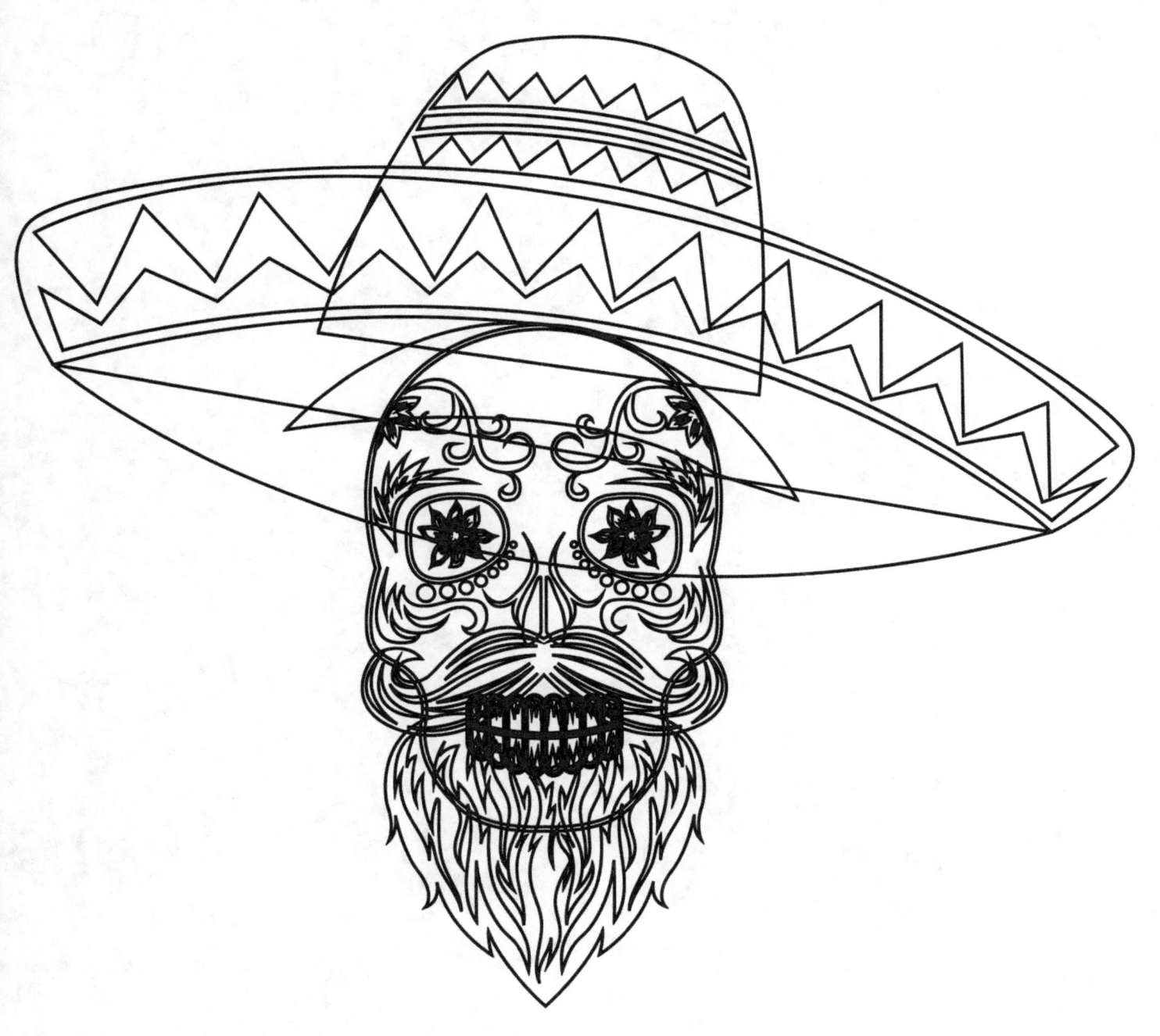

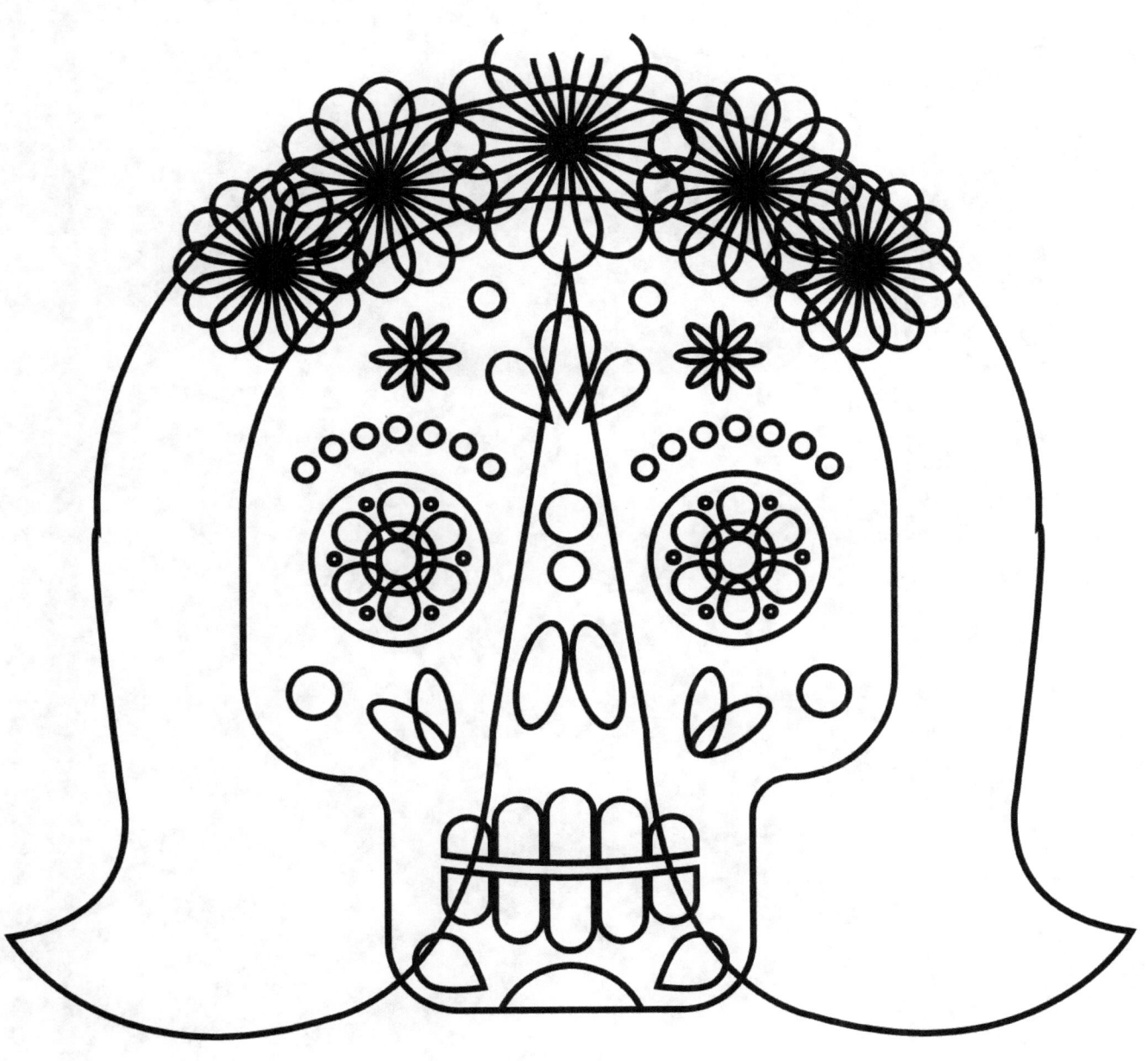

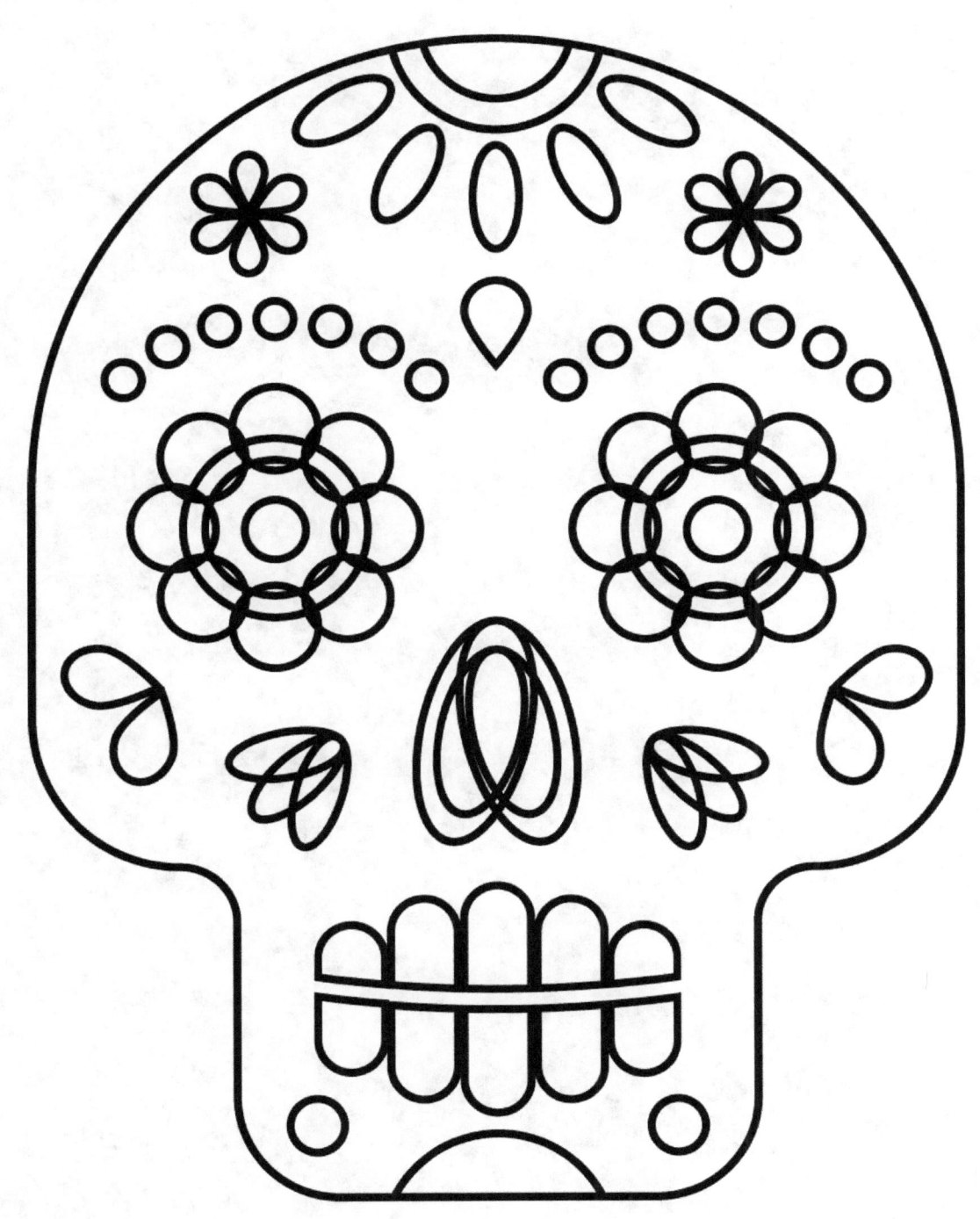

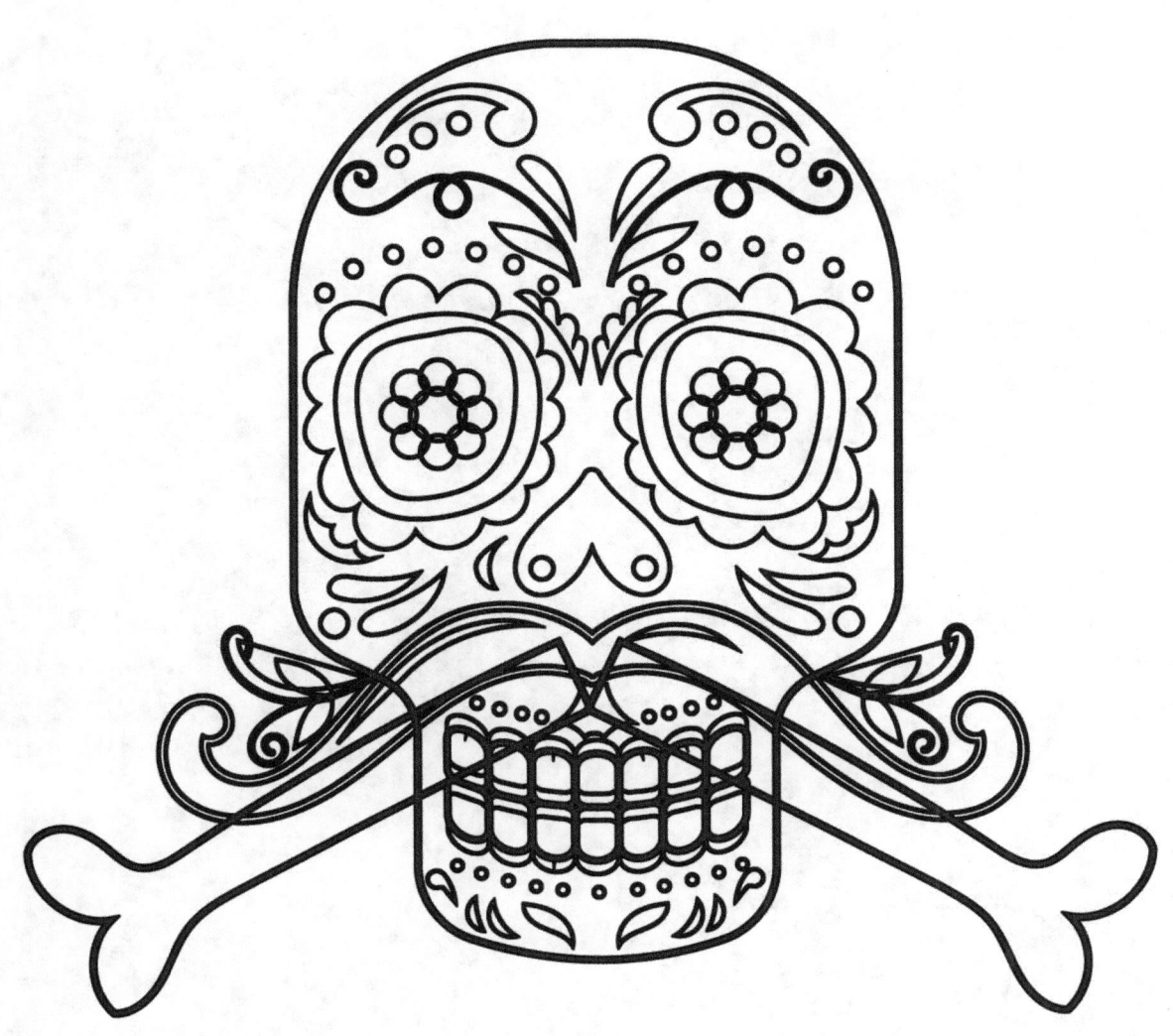

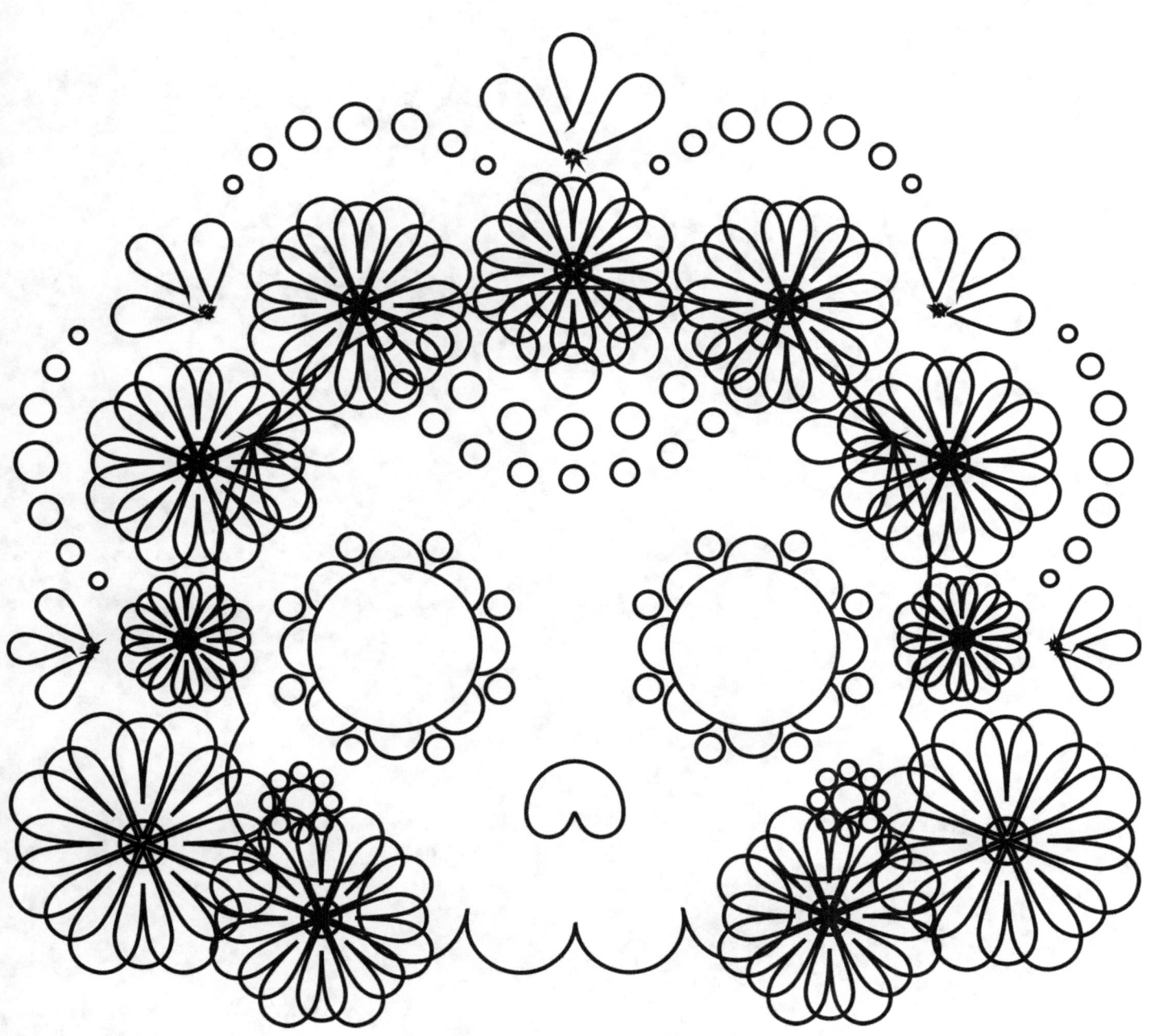

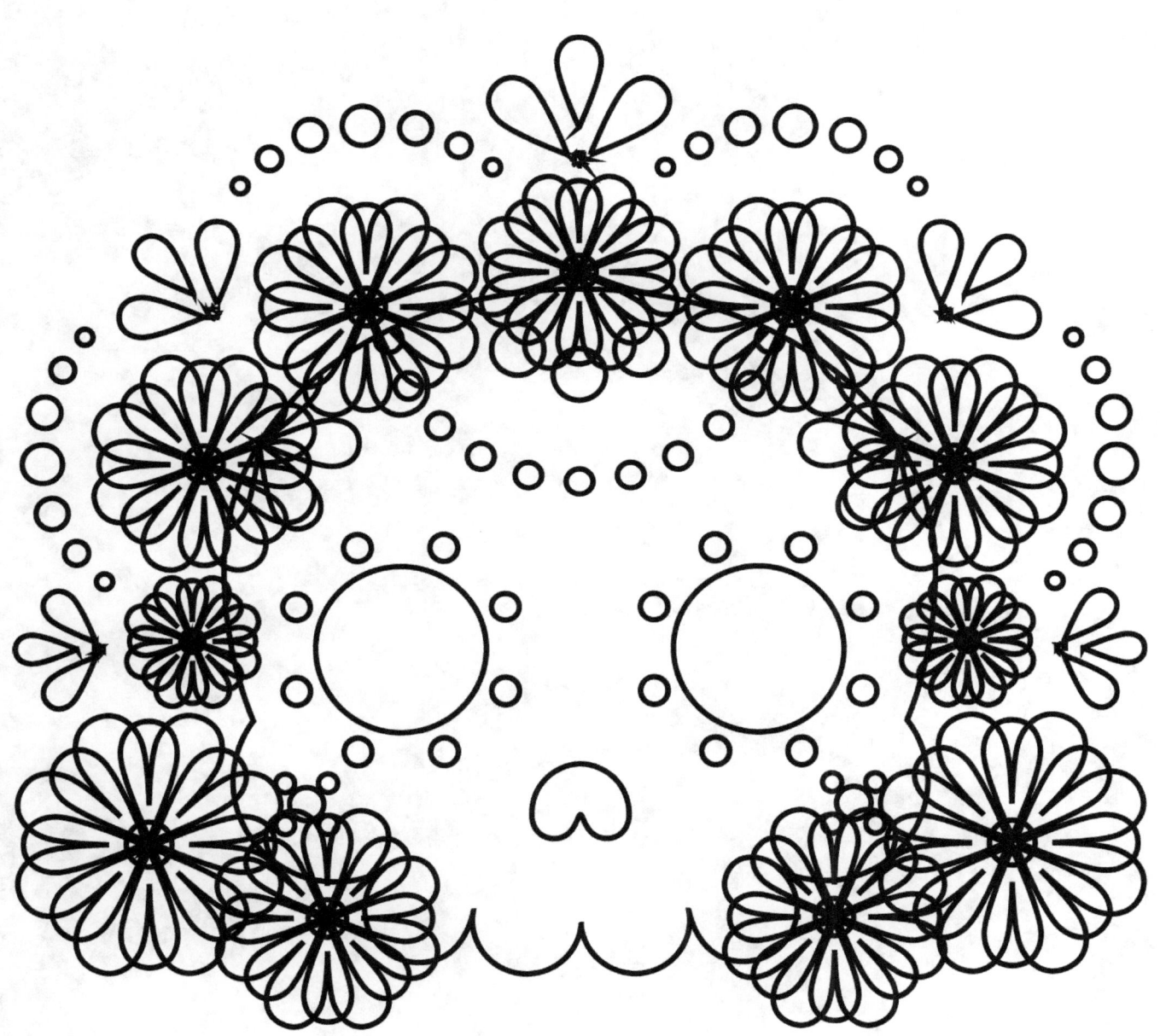

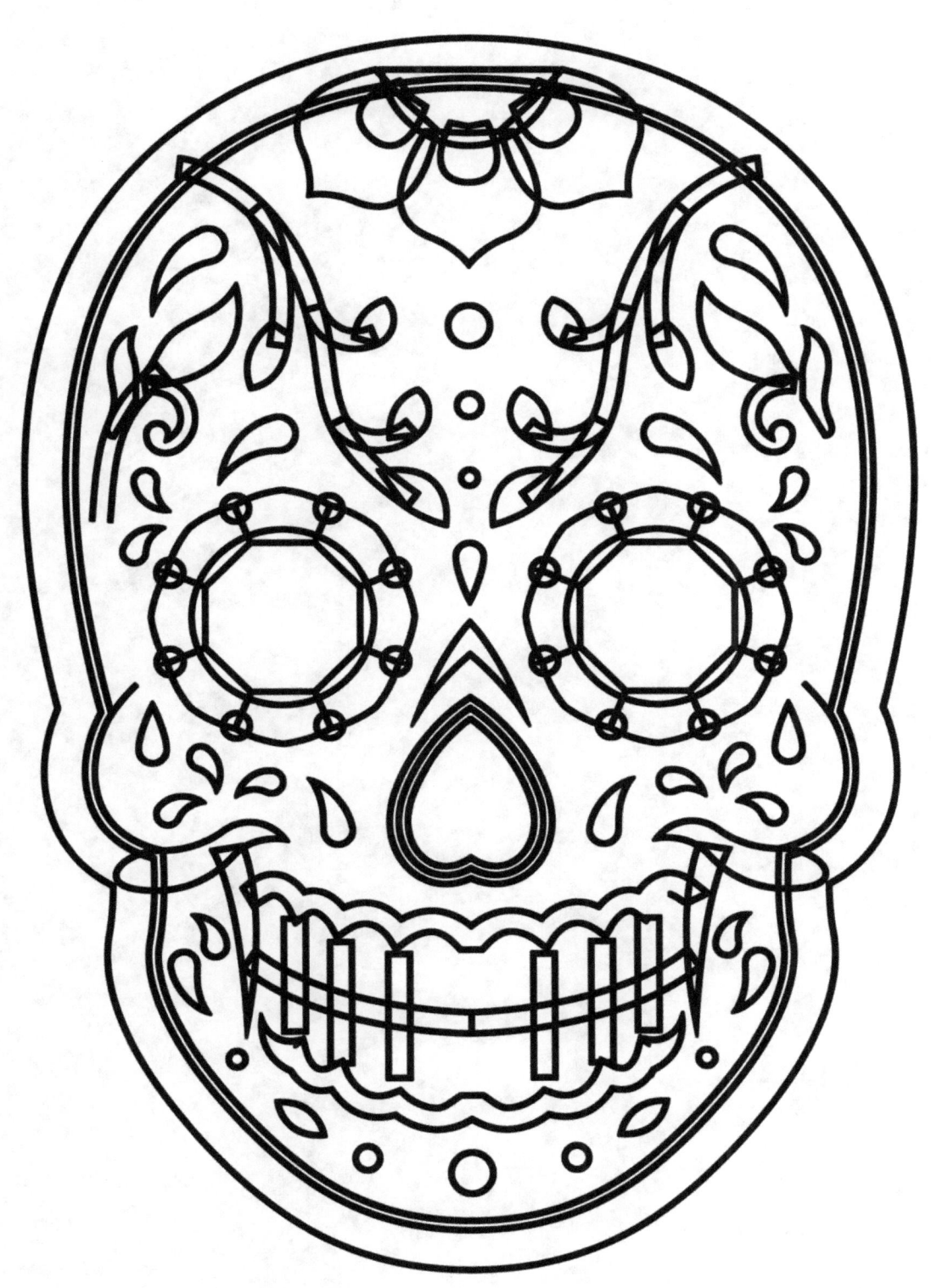

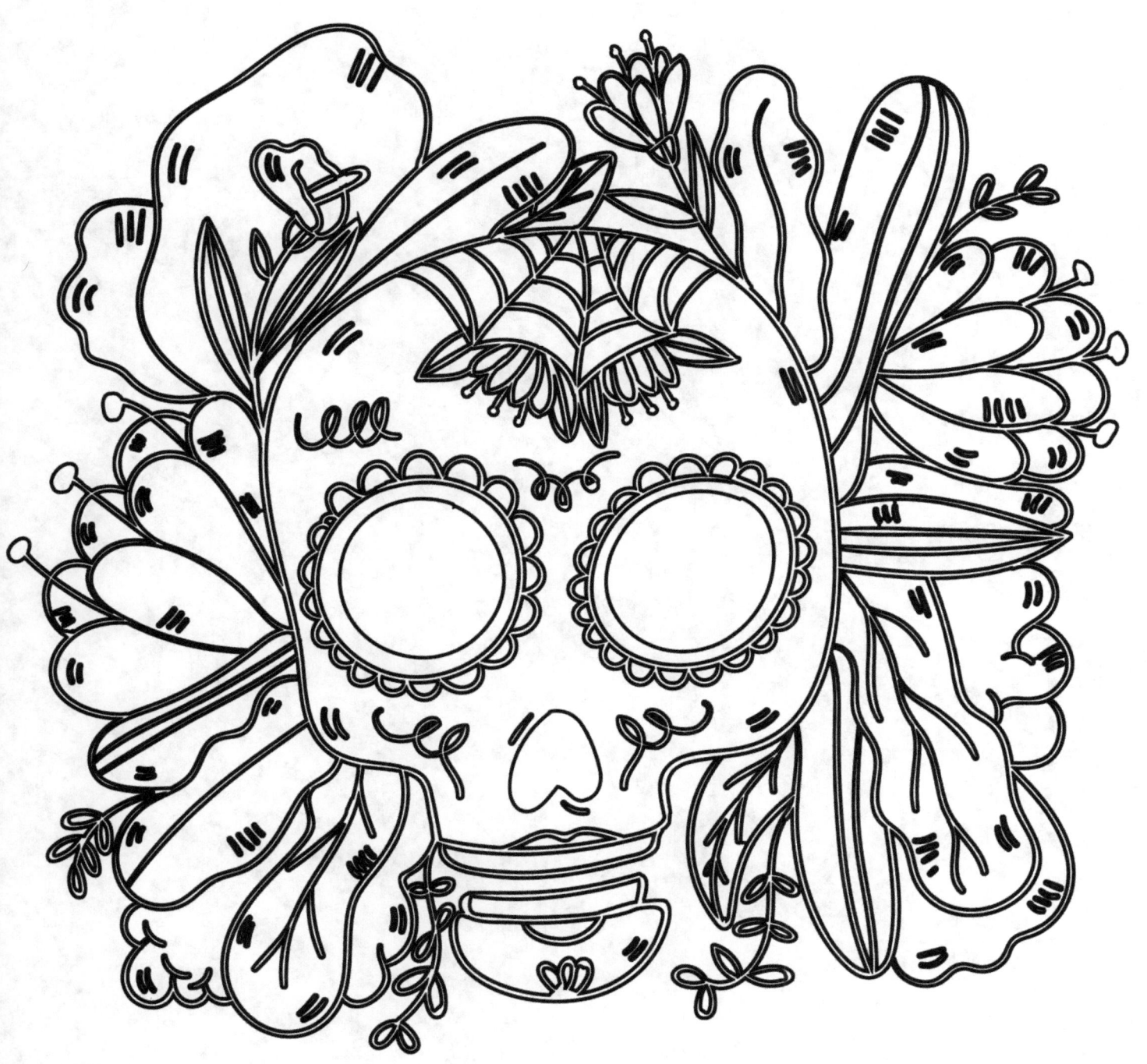

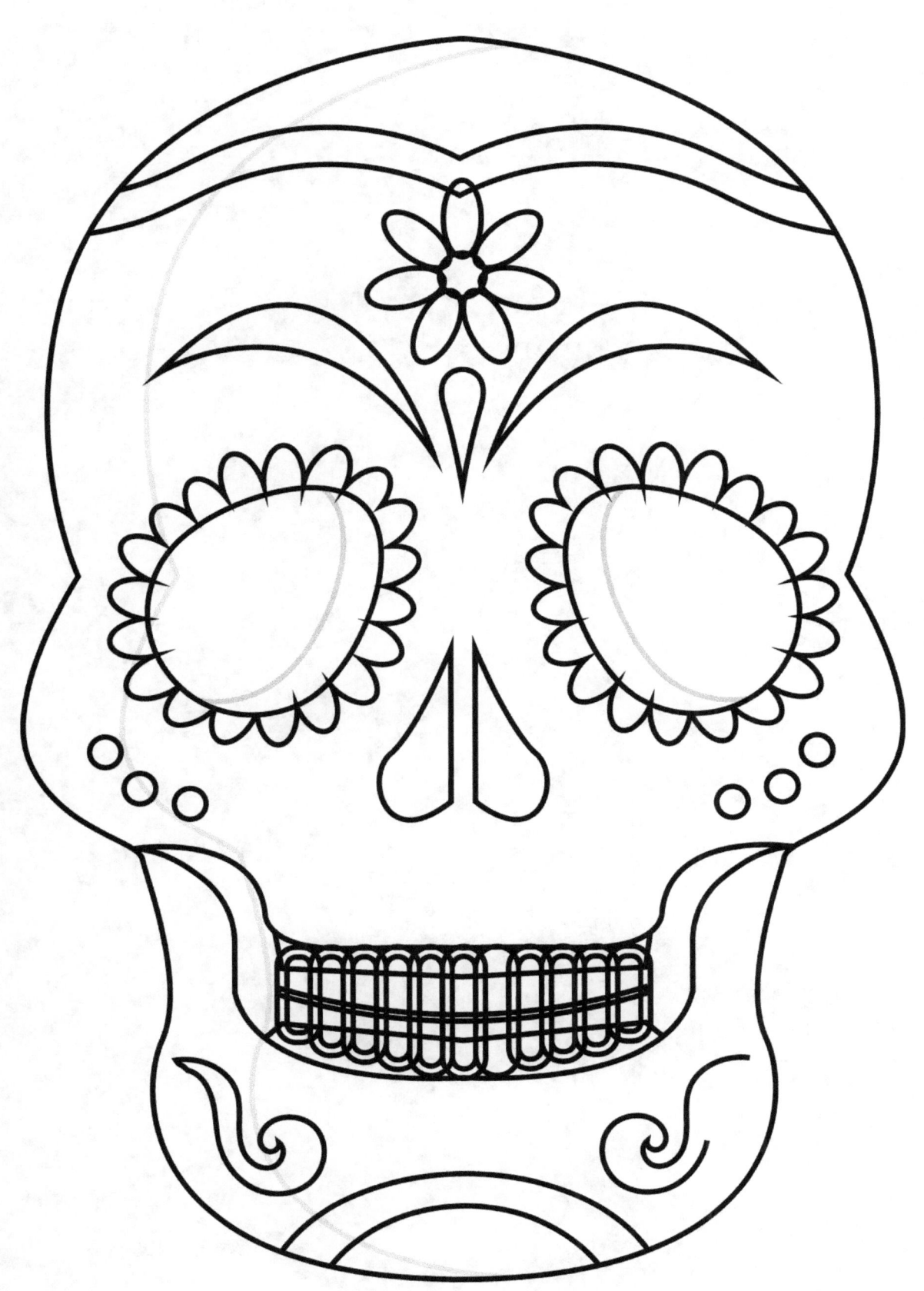

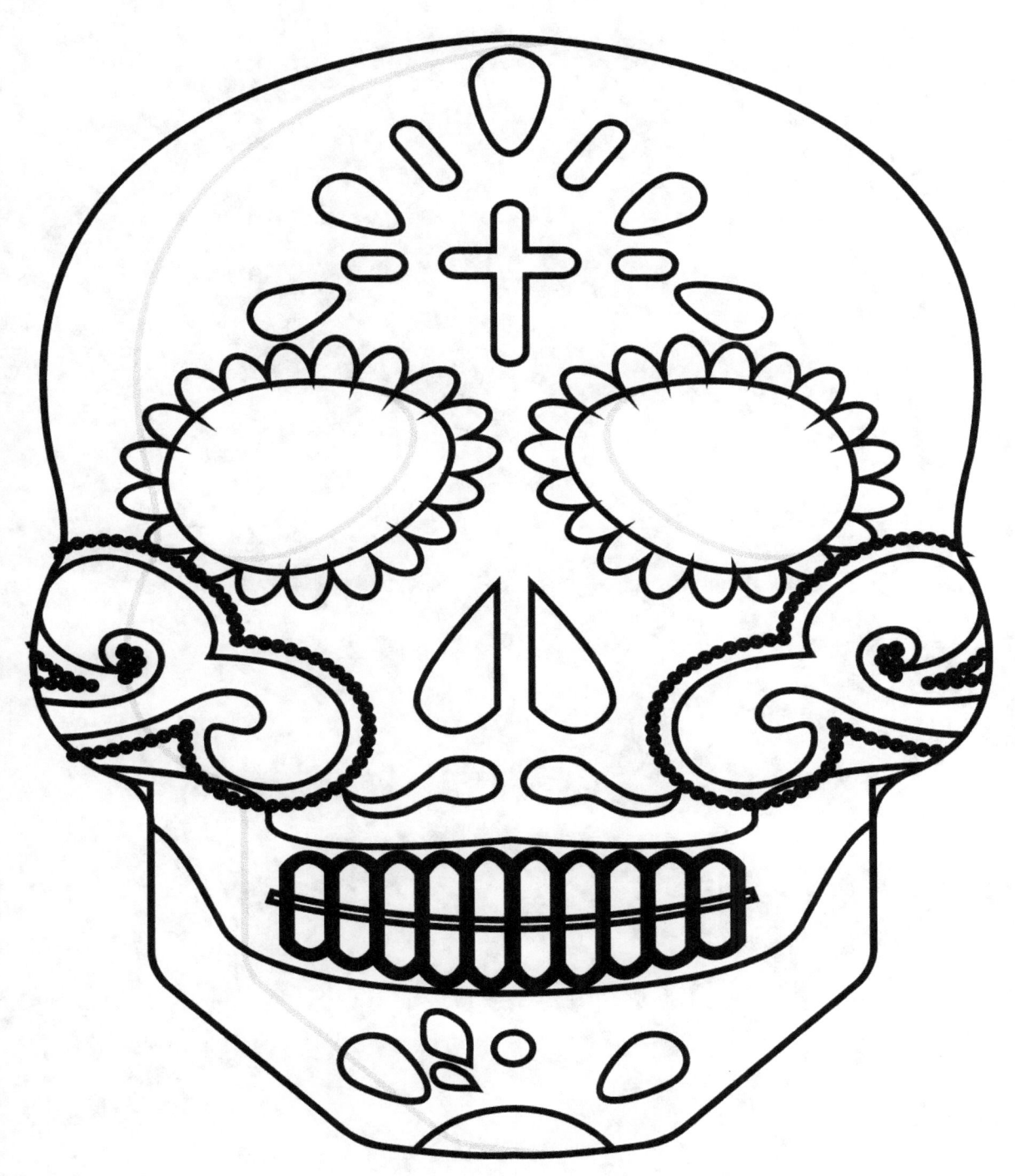

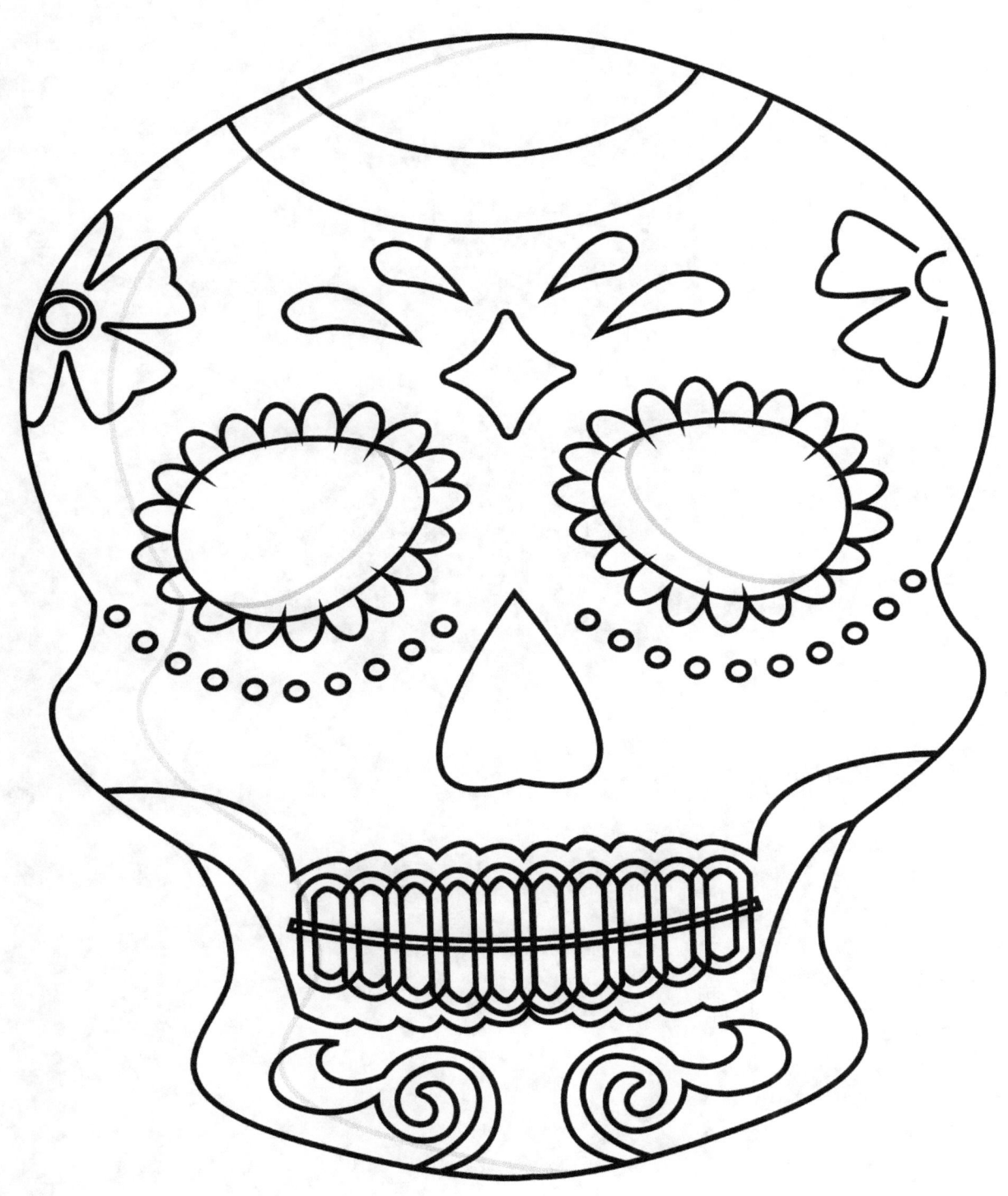

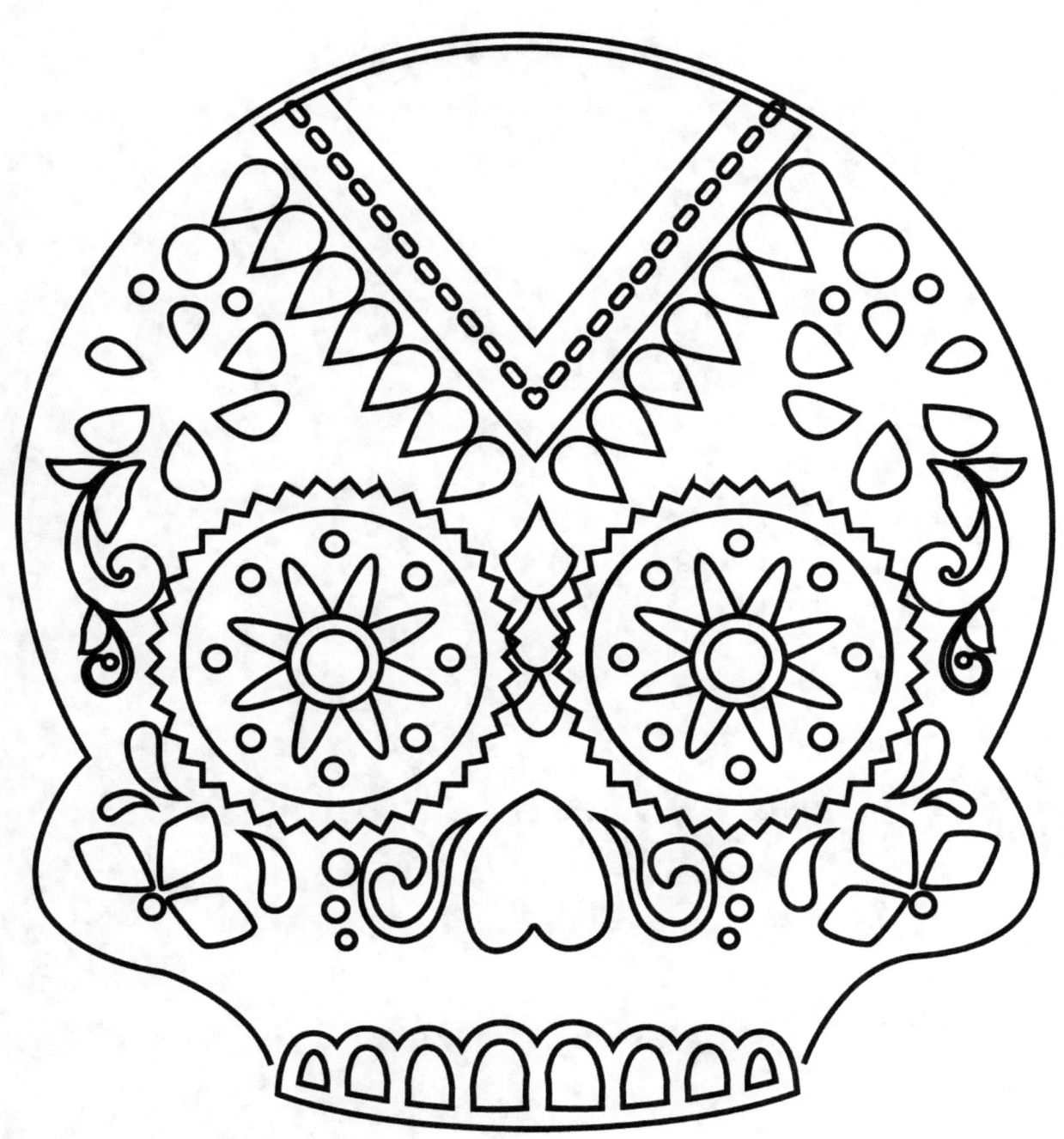

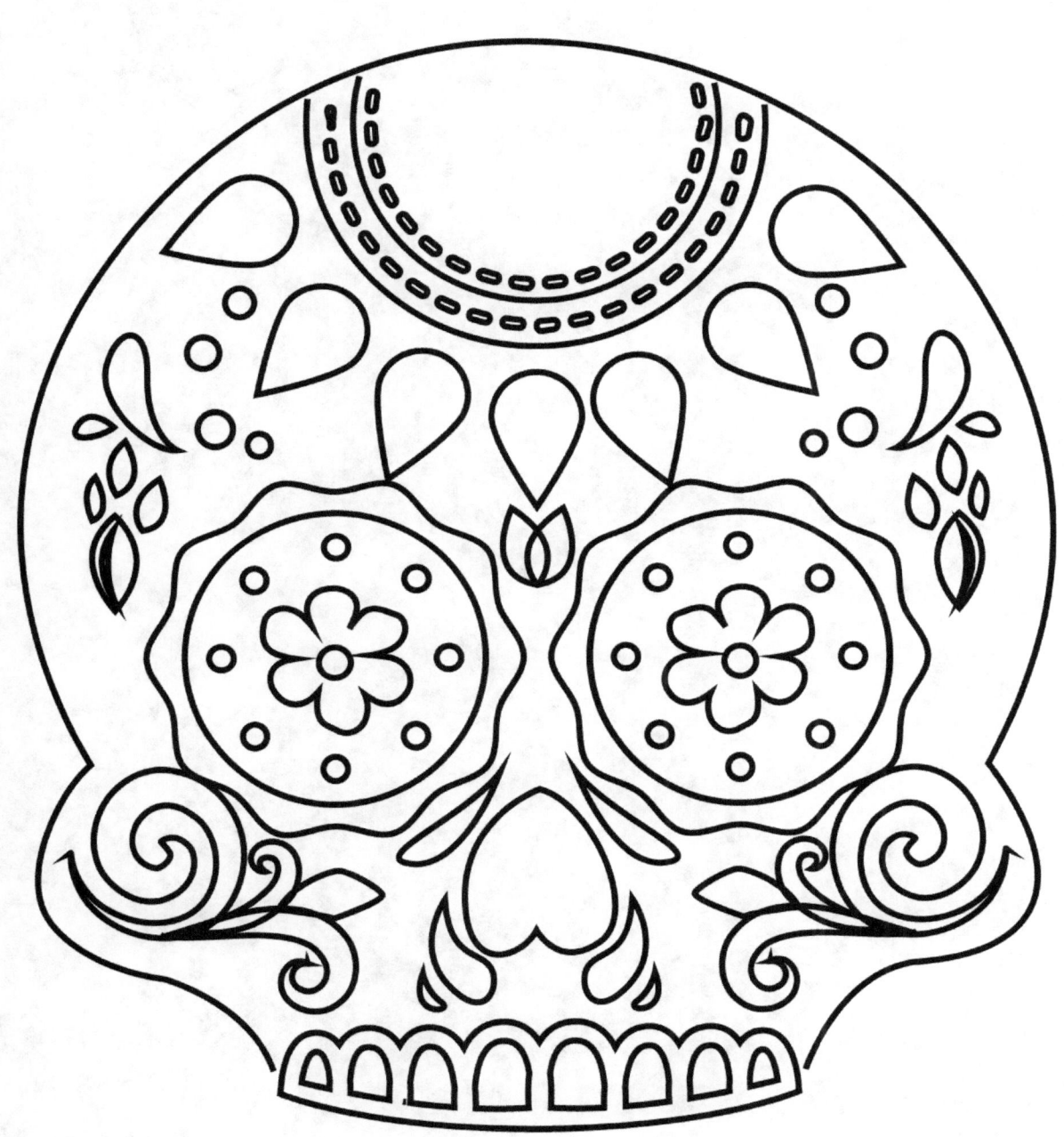

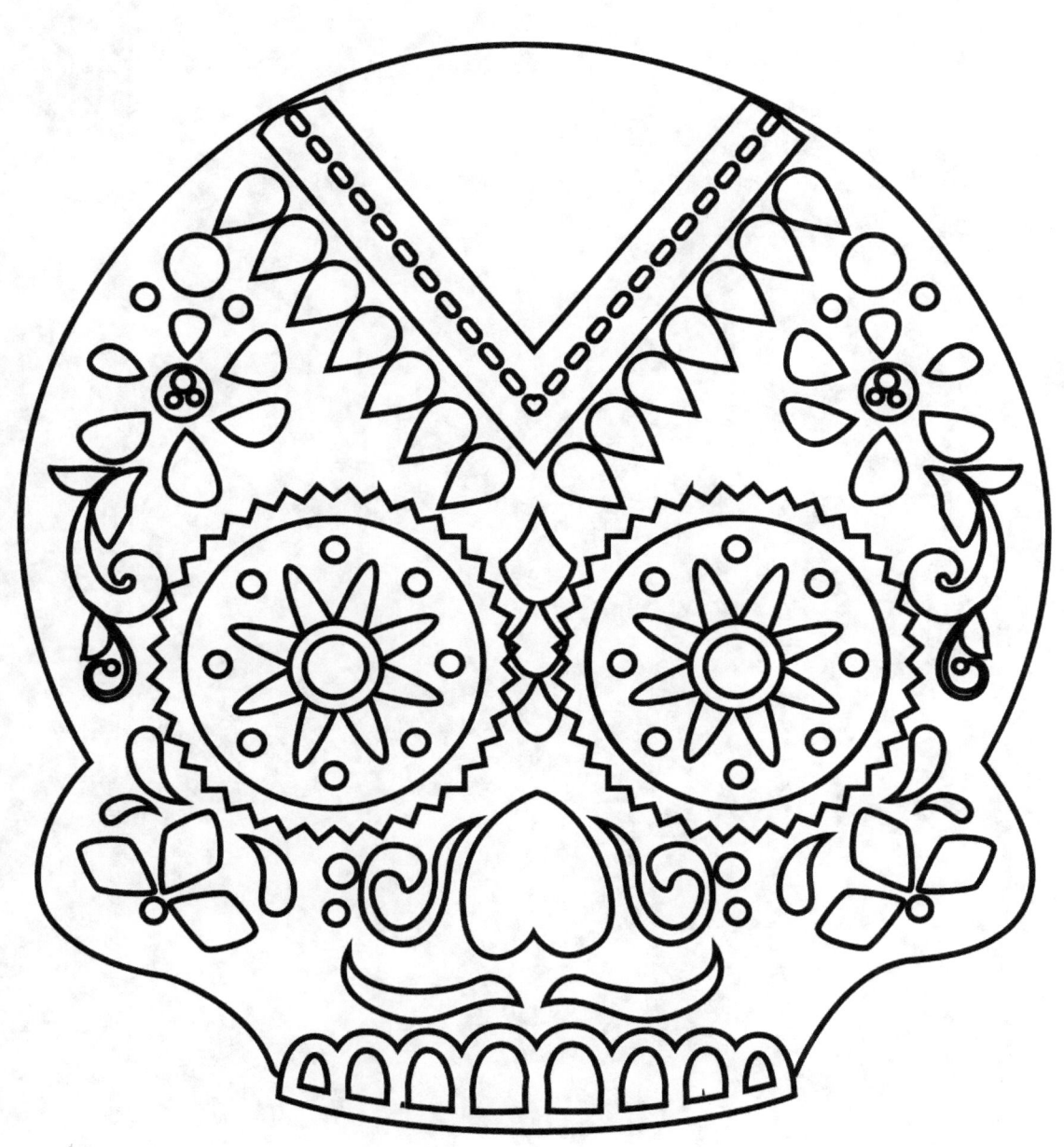

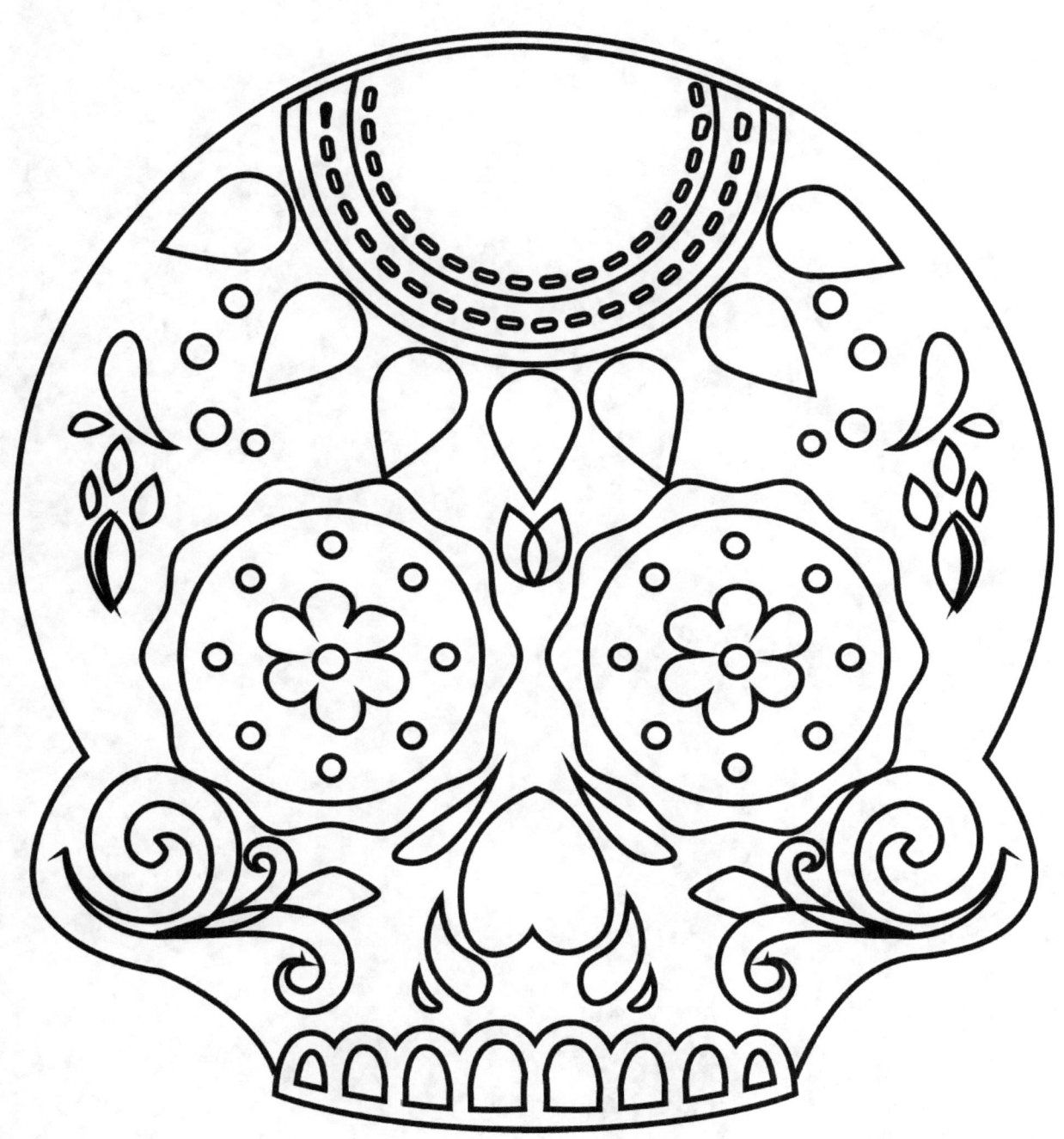

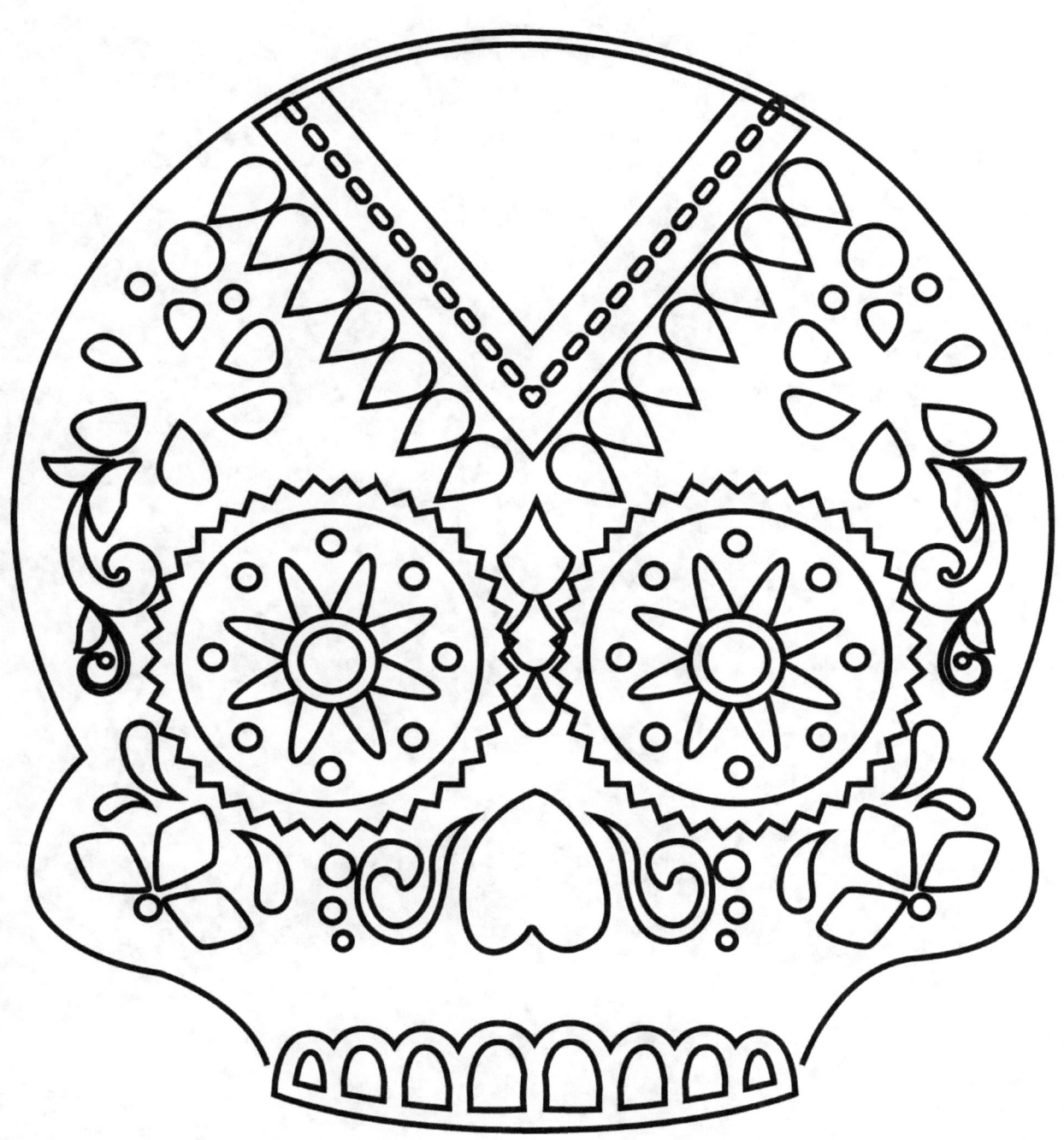

www.ingramcontent.com/pod-product-compliance
Lightning Source LLC
Chambersburg PA
CBHW060438220526
45465CB00008B/3182